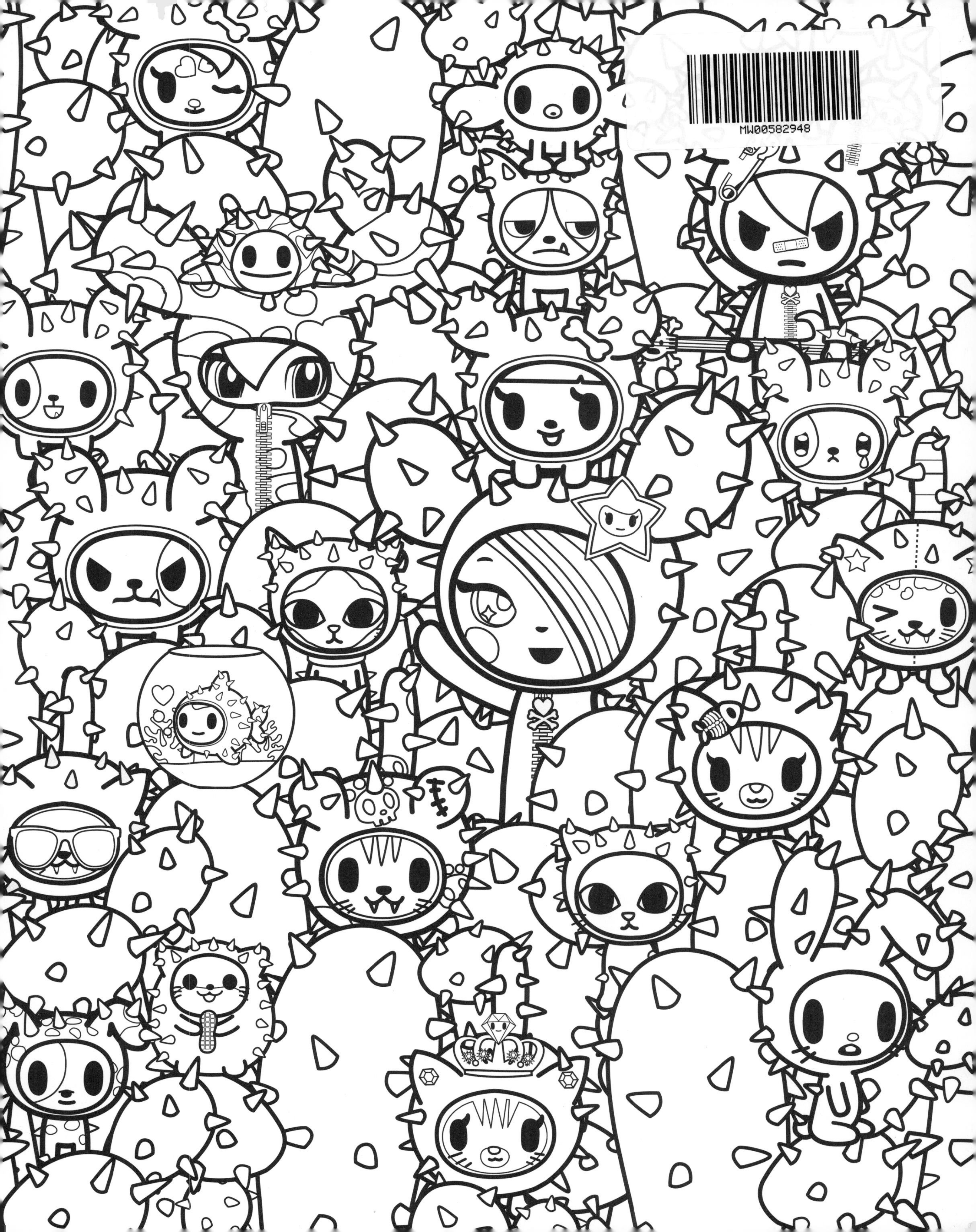

POPCORN

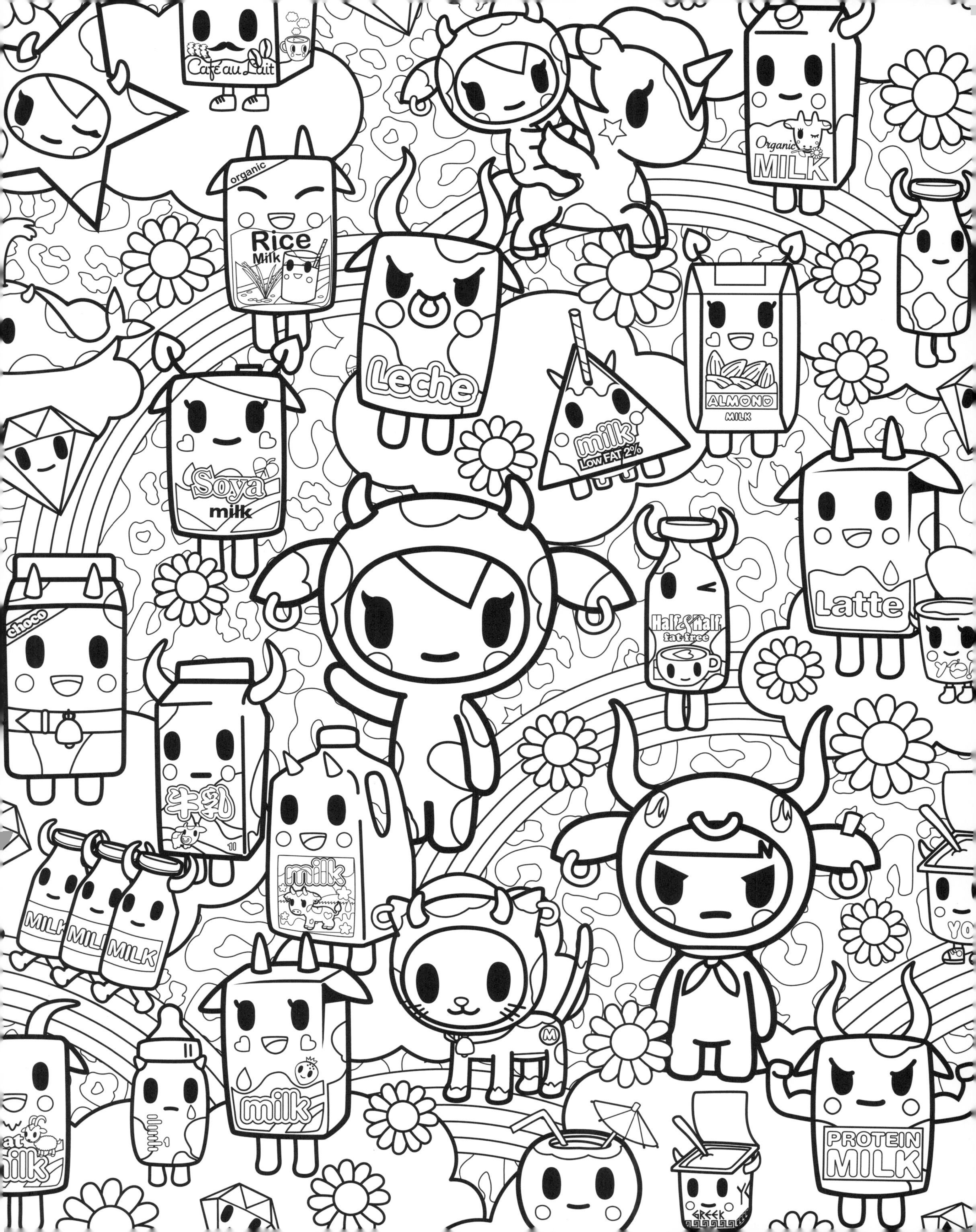

Café au Lait
organic
Rice
Milk
Leche
Organic
MILK
ALMOND
MILK
milk
Low FAT 2%
Soya
milk
choco
Latte
Half&Half
fat-free
牛乳
milk
MILK
milk
PROTEIN
MILK
GREEK

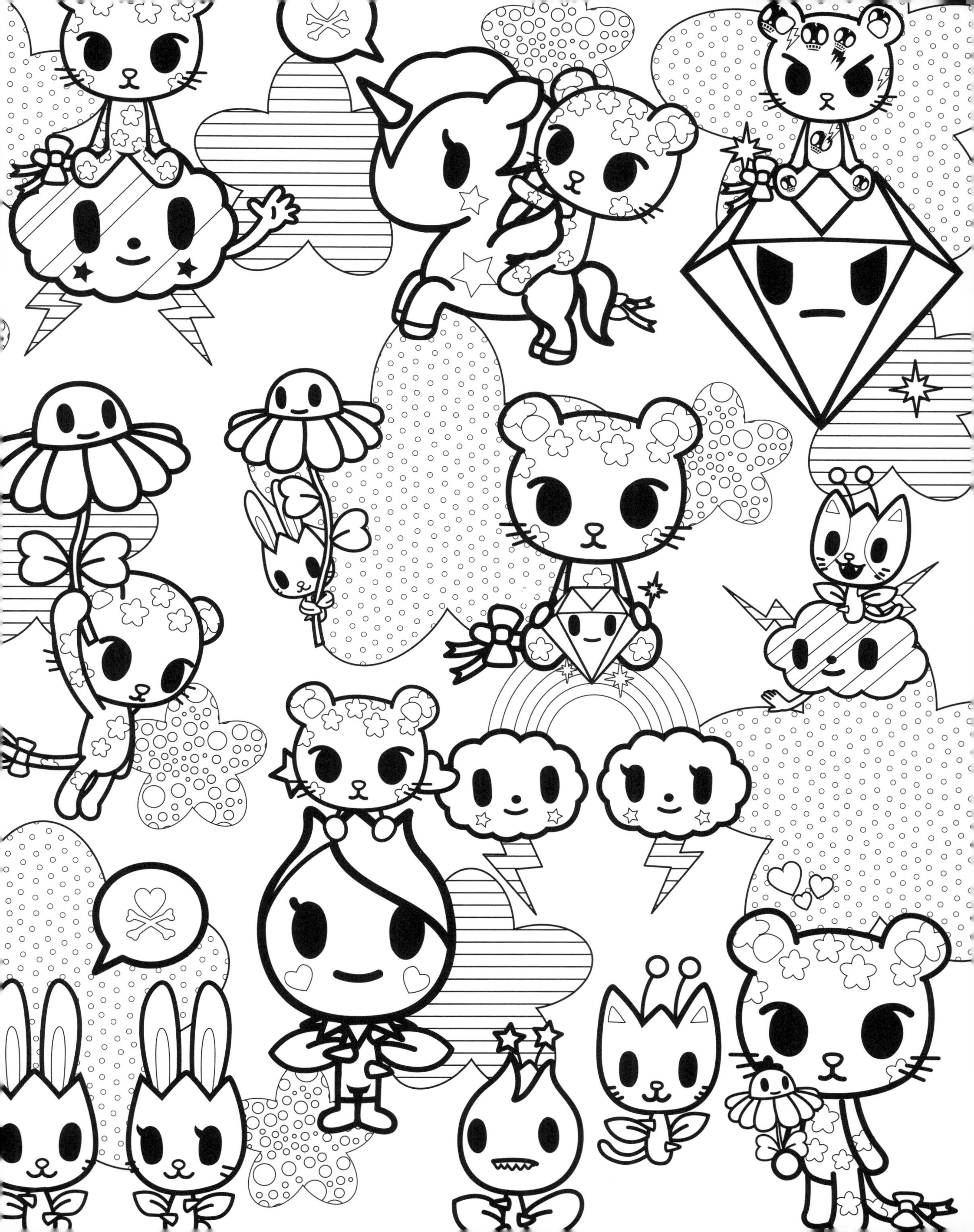

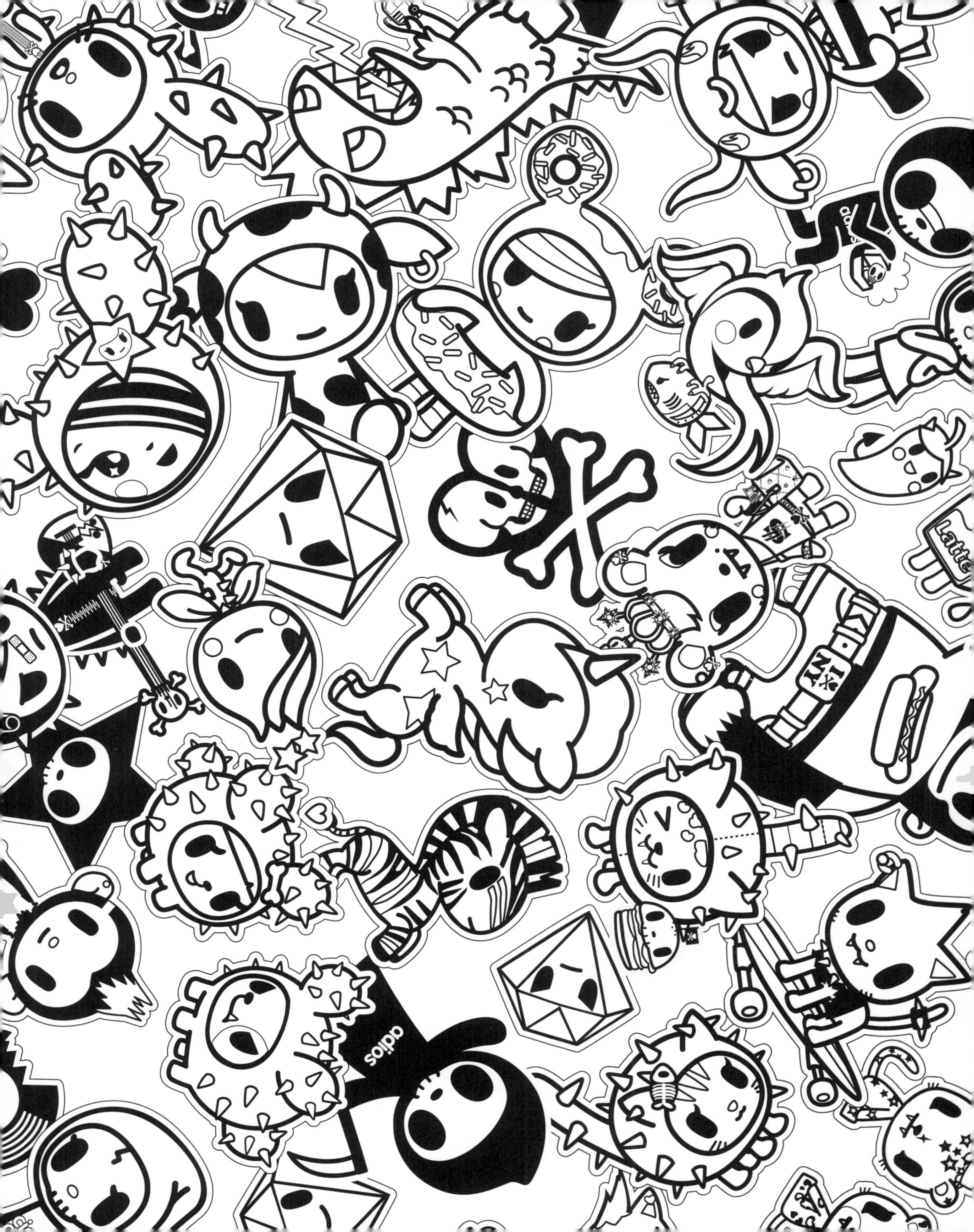
Latte
adios

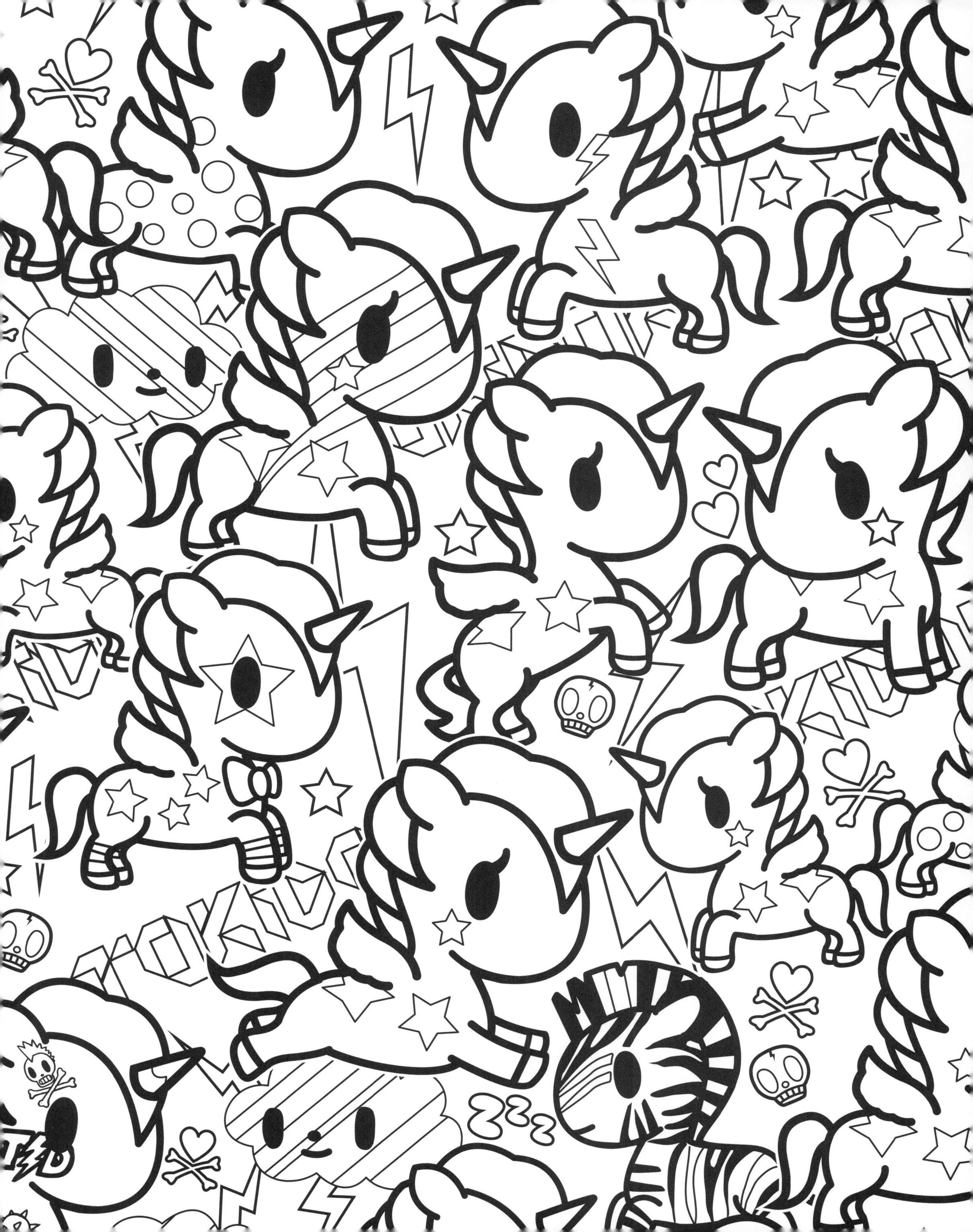
ZZZ

POPCORN

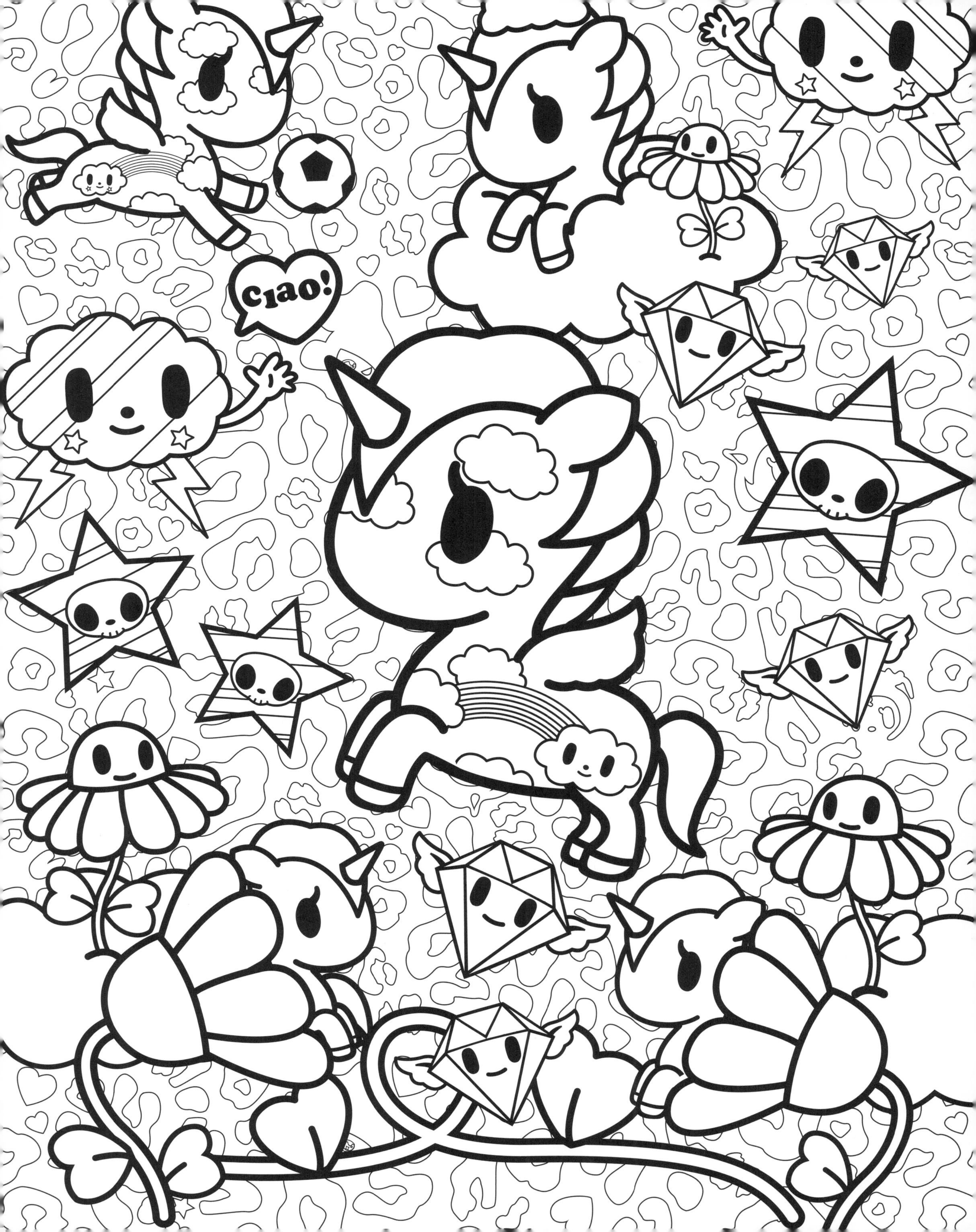
ciao!

Soya
milk
Latte

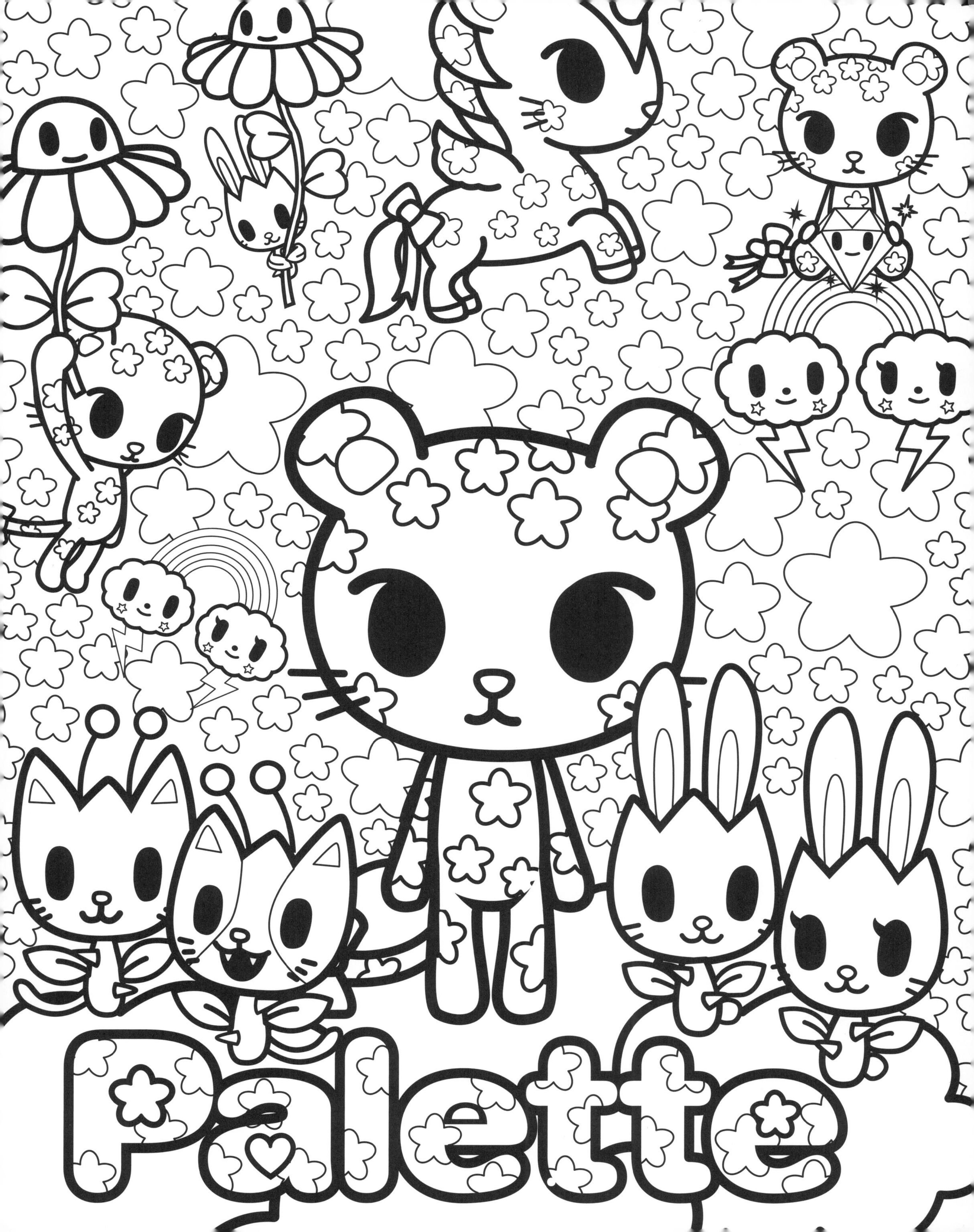
Palette

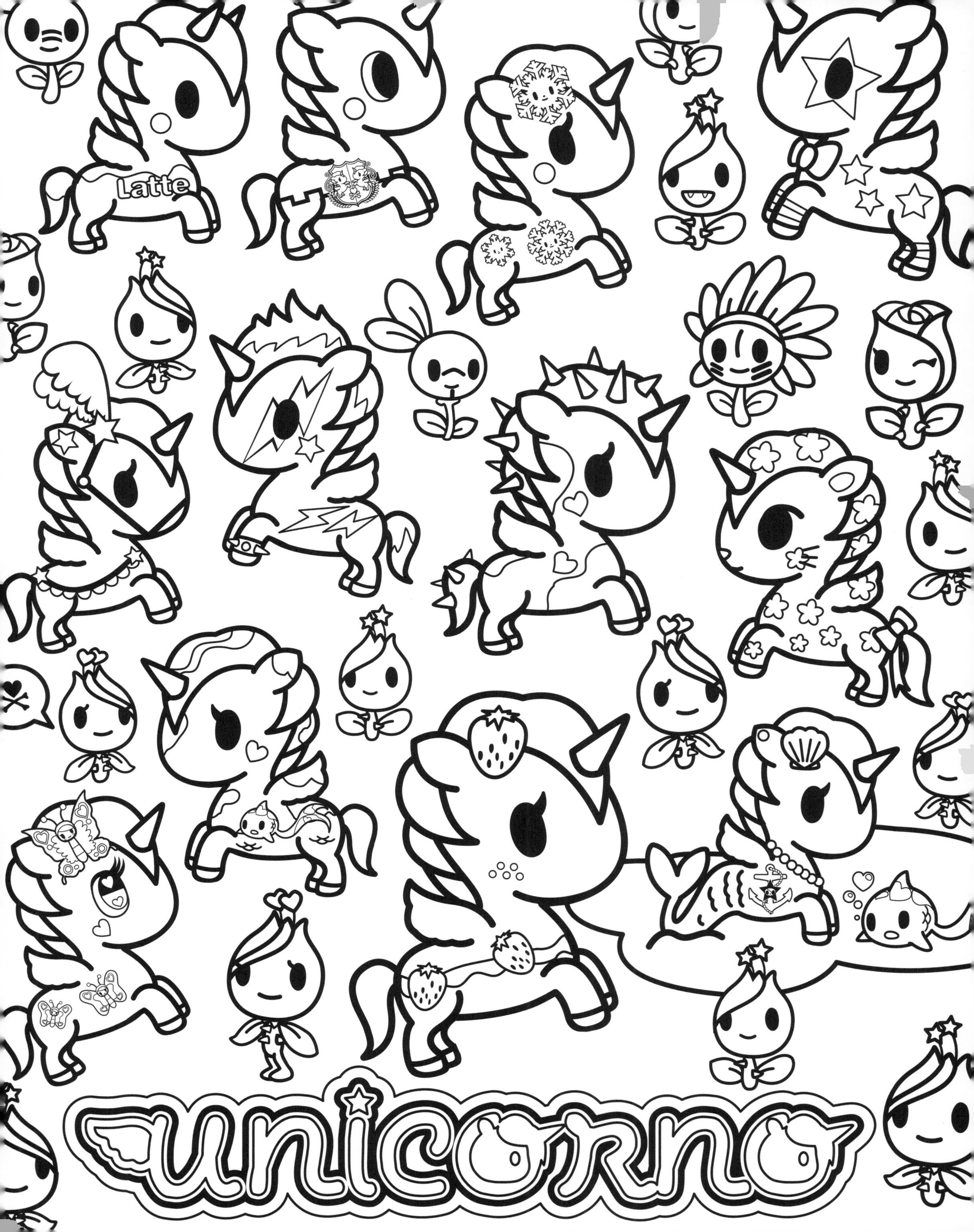
Latte
unicorno

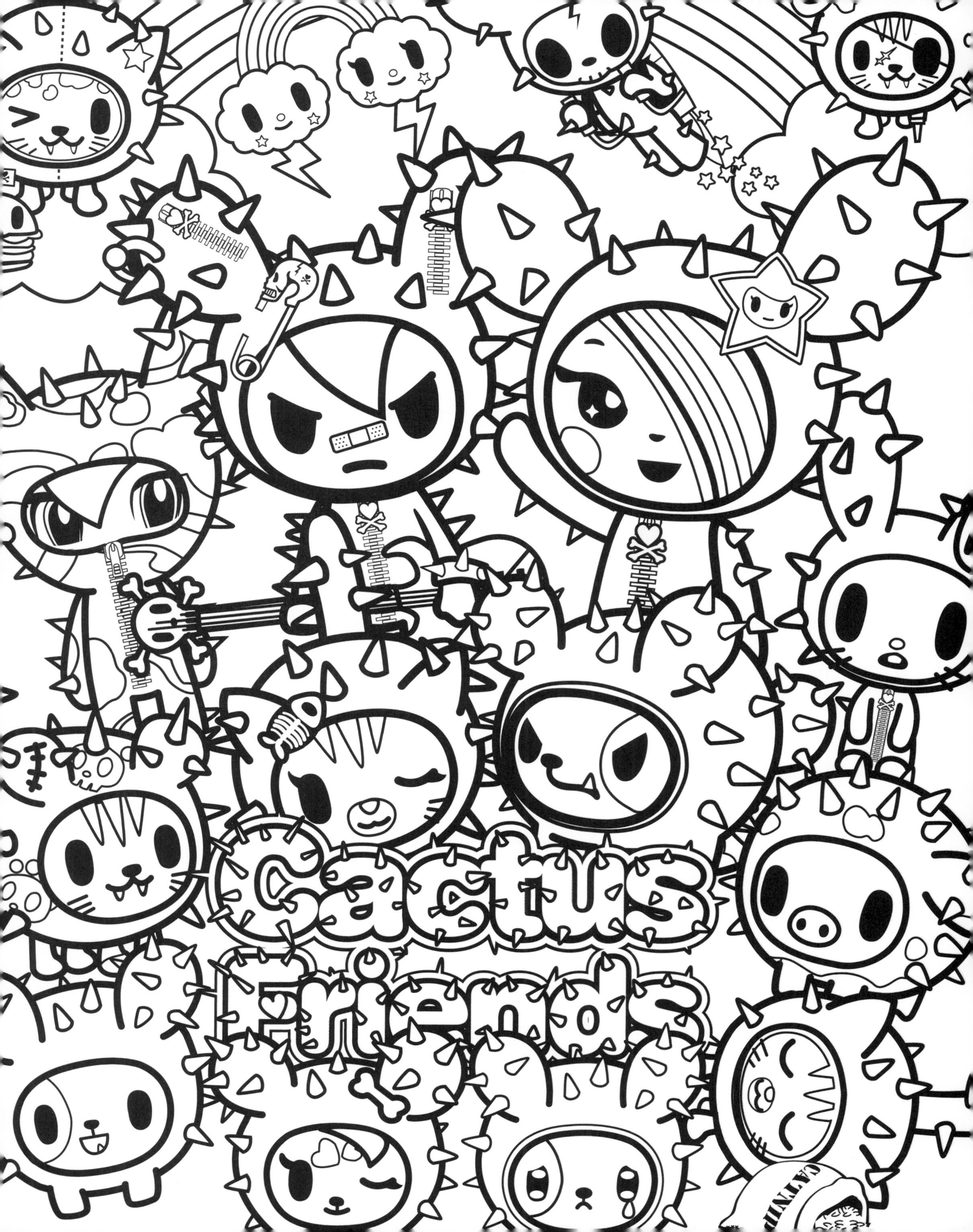
cactus
friends

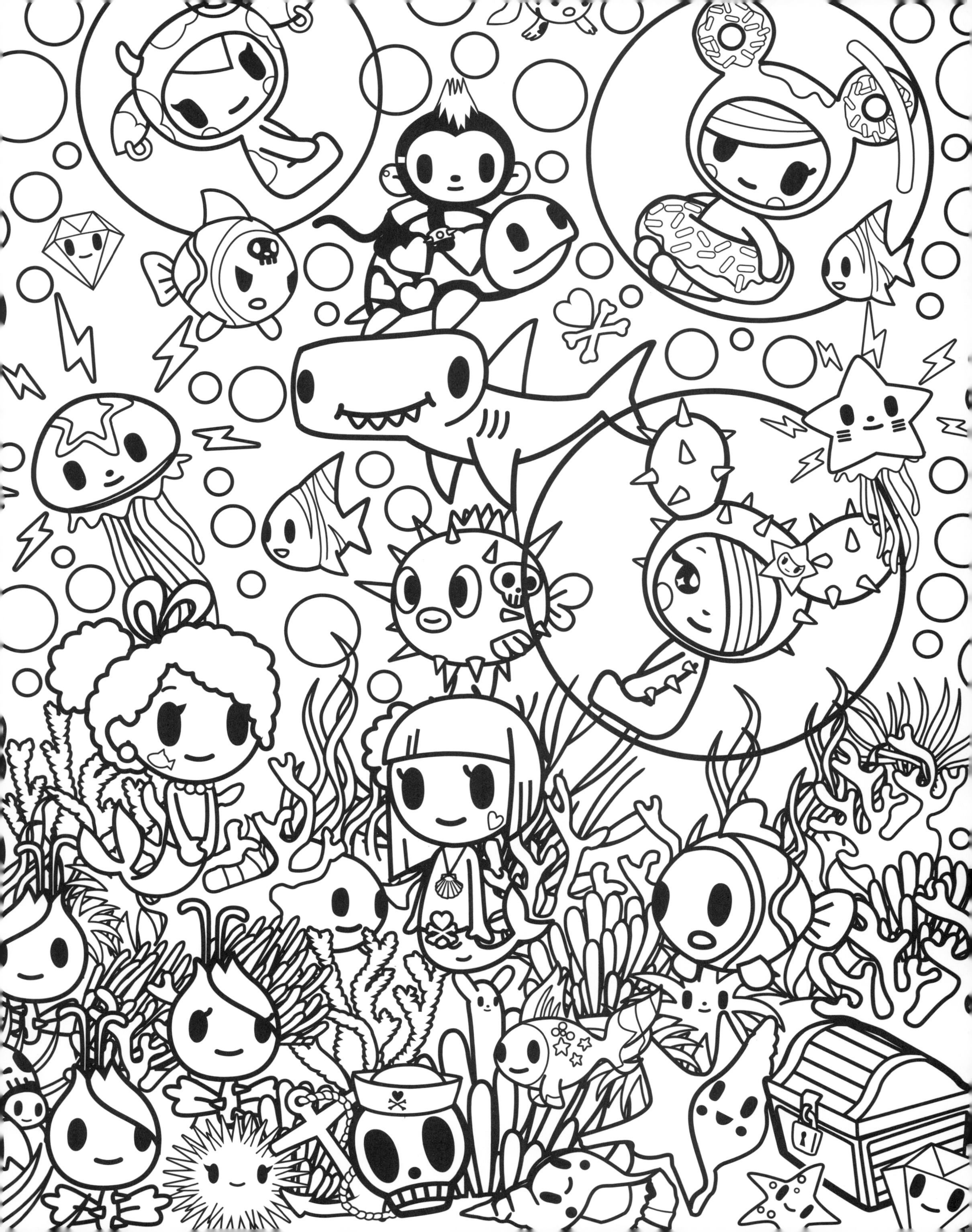

TOKIDOKI
SEAFOOD
adios

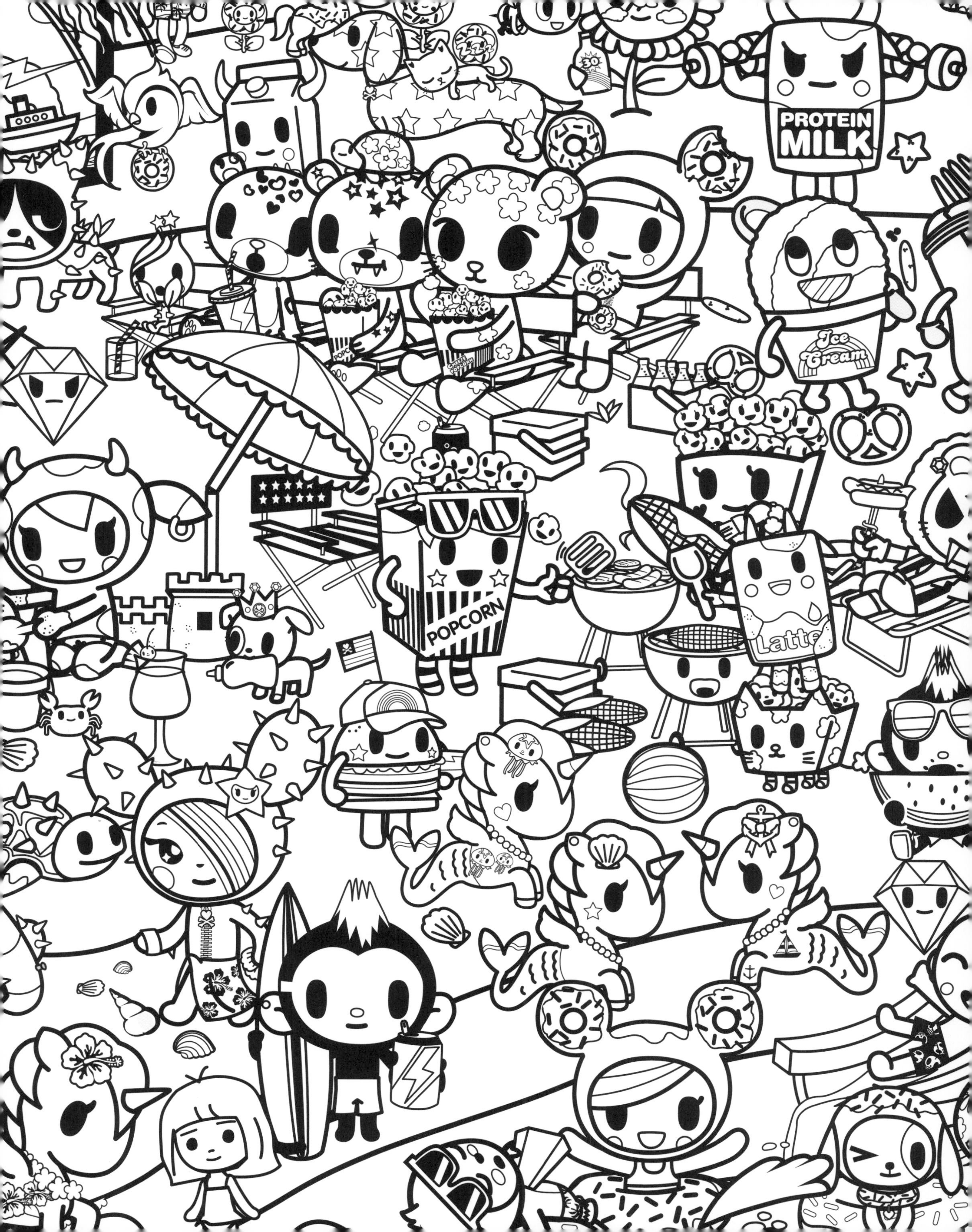
PROTEIN
MILK
Ice
Cream
POPCORN
Latte

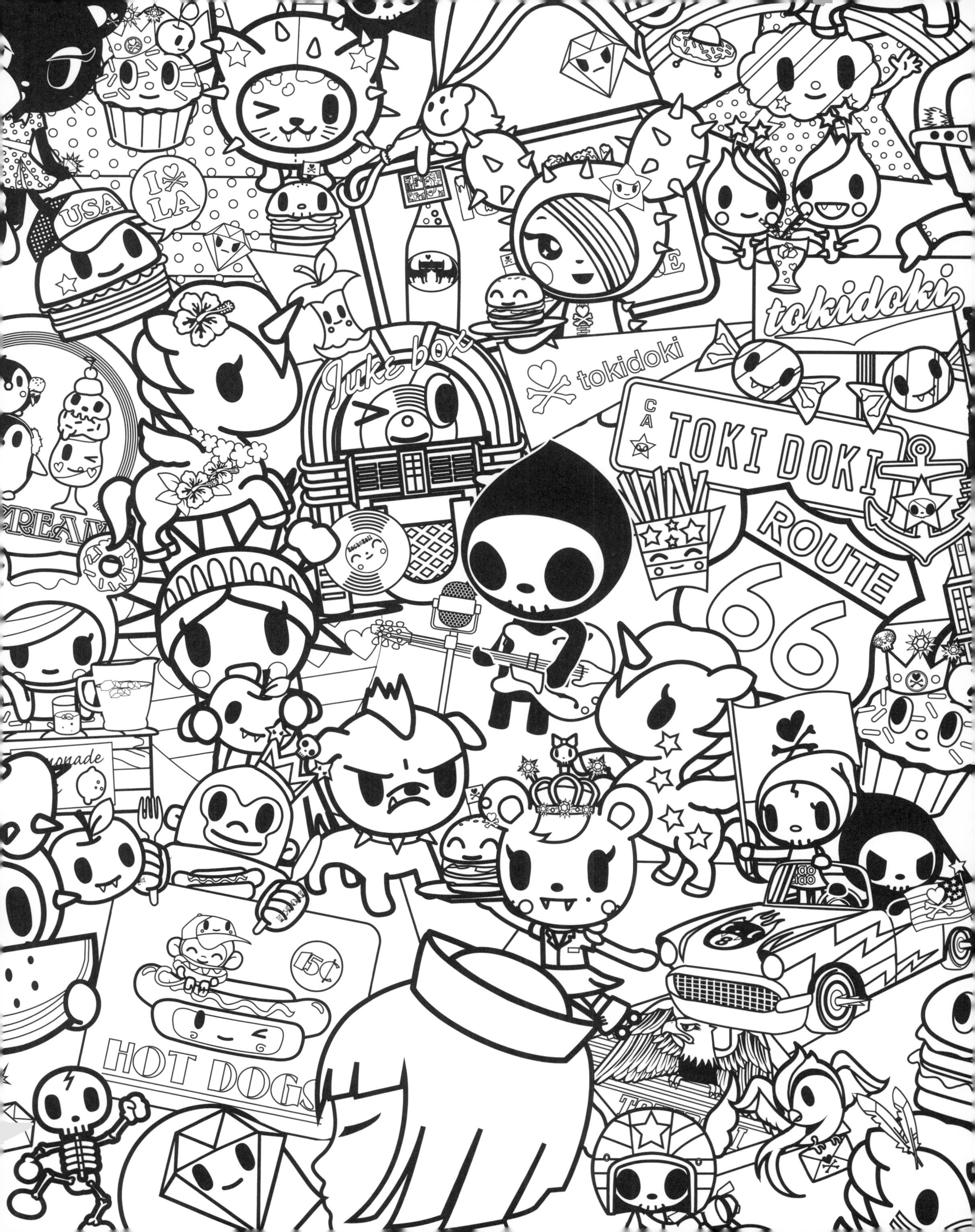
USA
tokidoki
Juke box
tokidoki
CA
TOKI DOKI
ROUTE
66
15¢
HOT DOGS

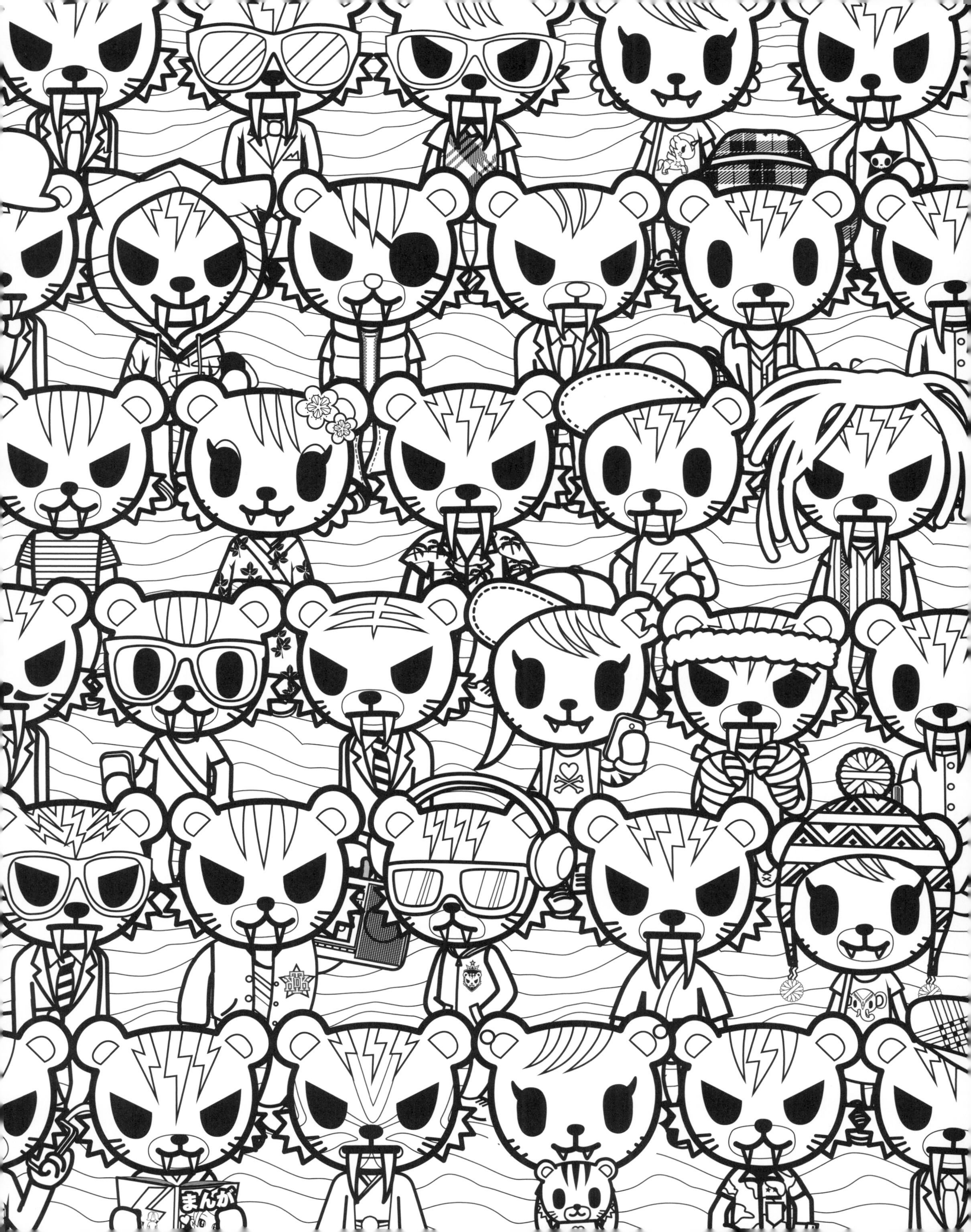
まんが

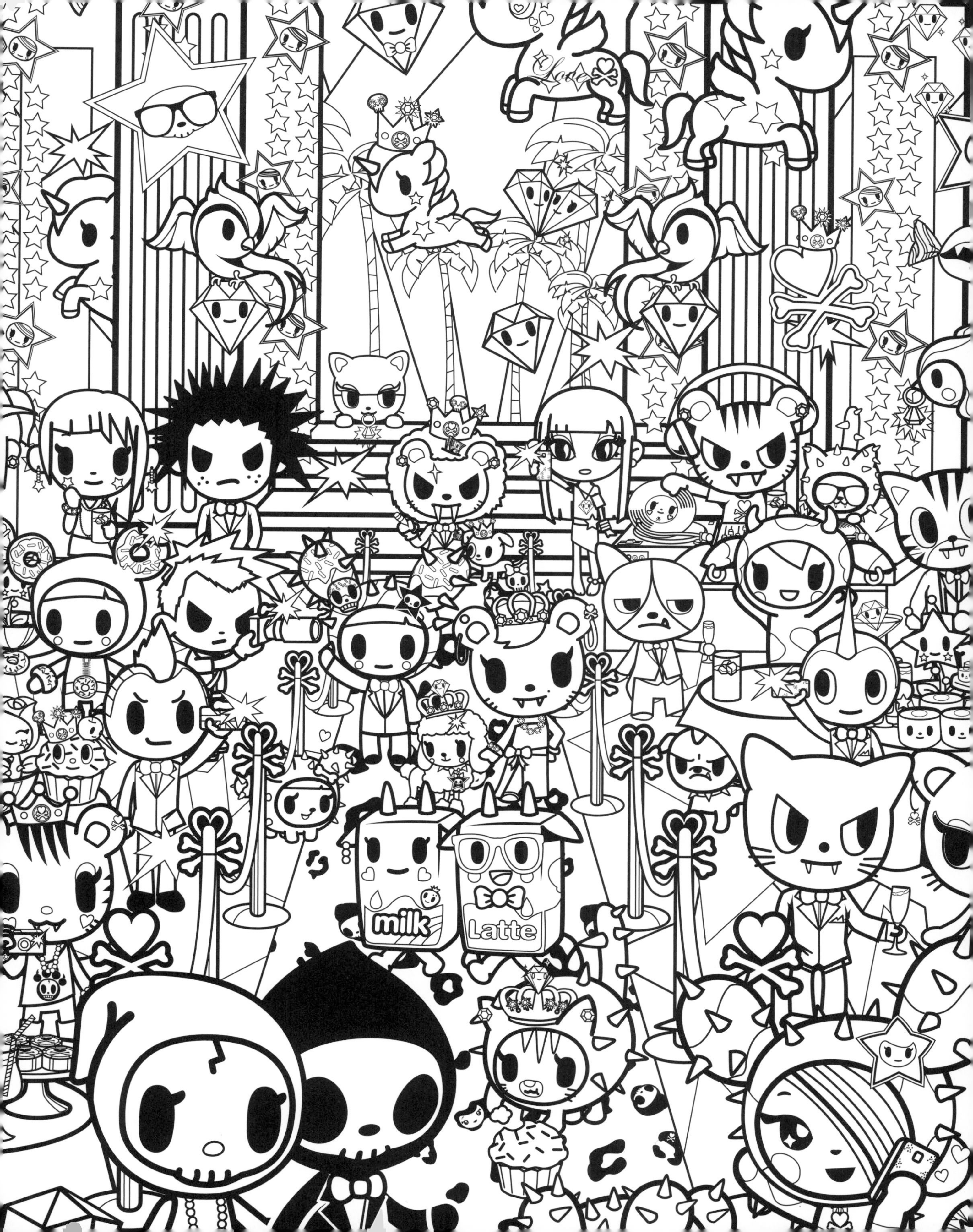
Love
milk
Latte

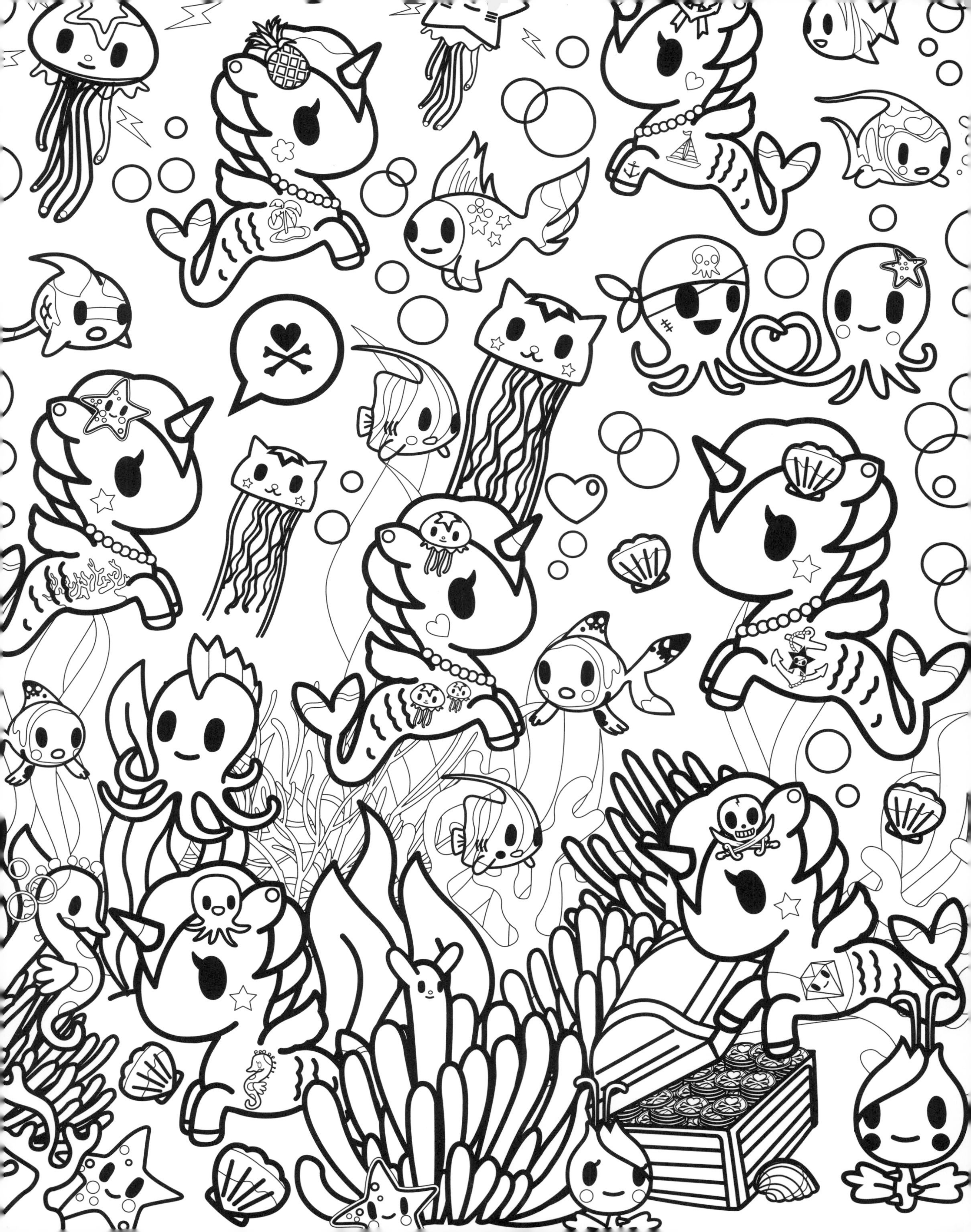

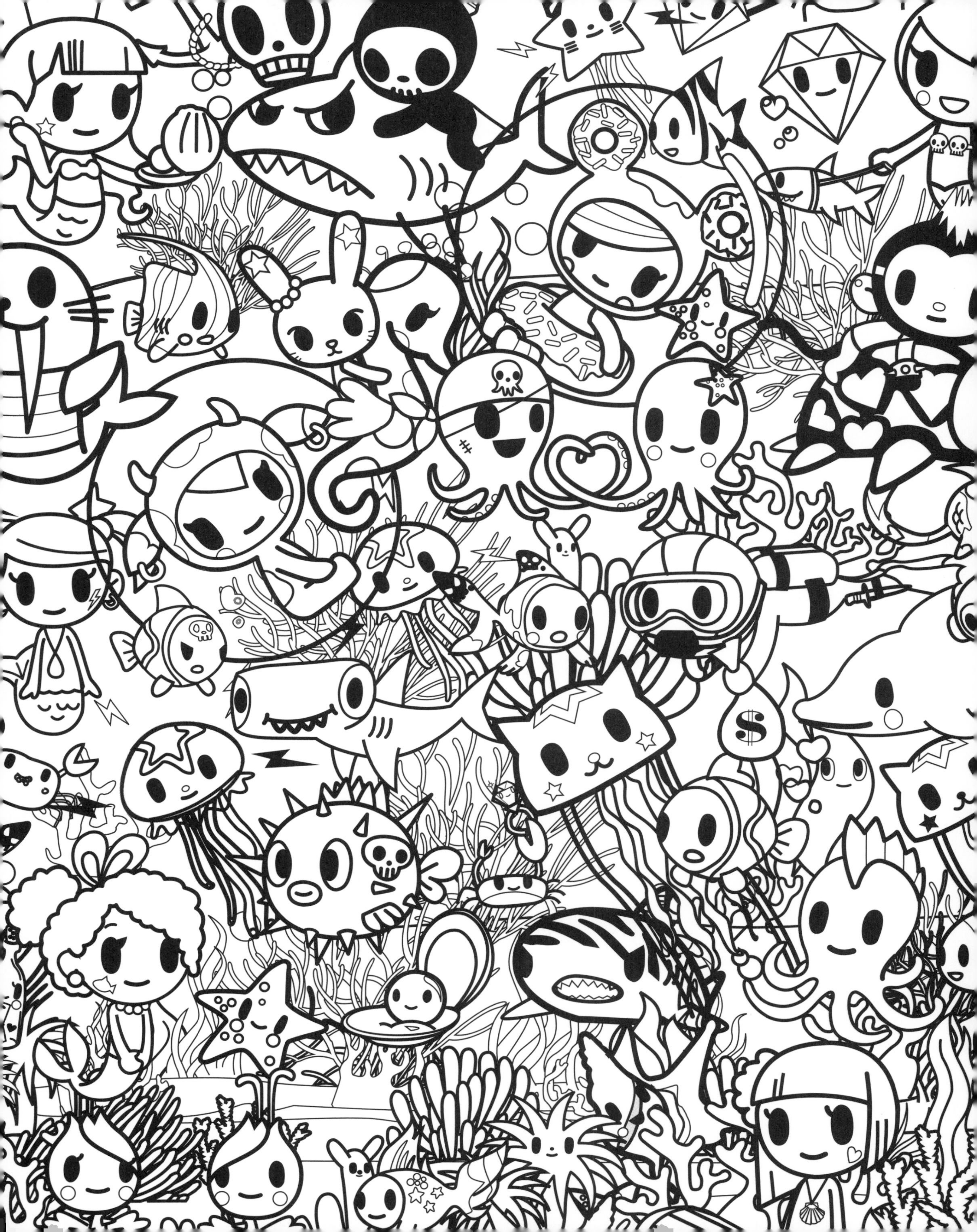

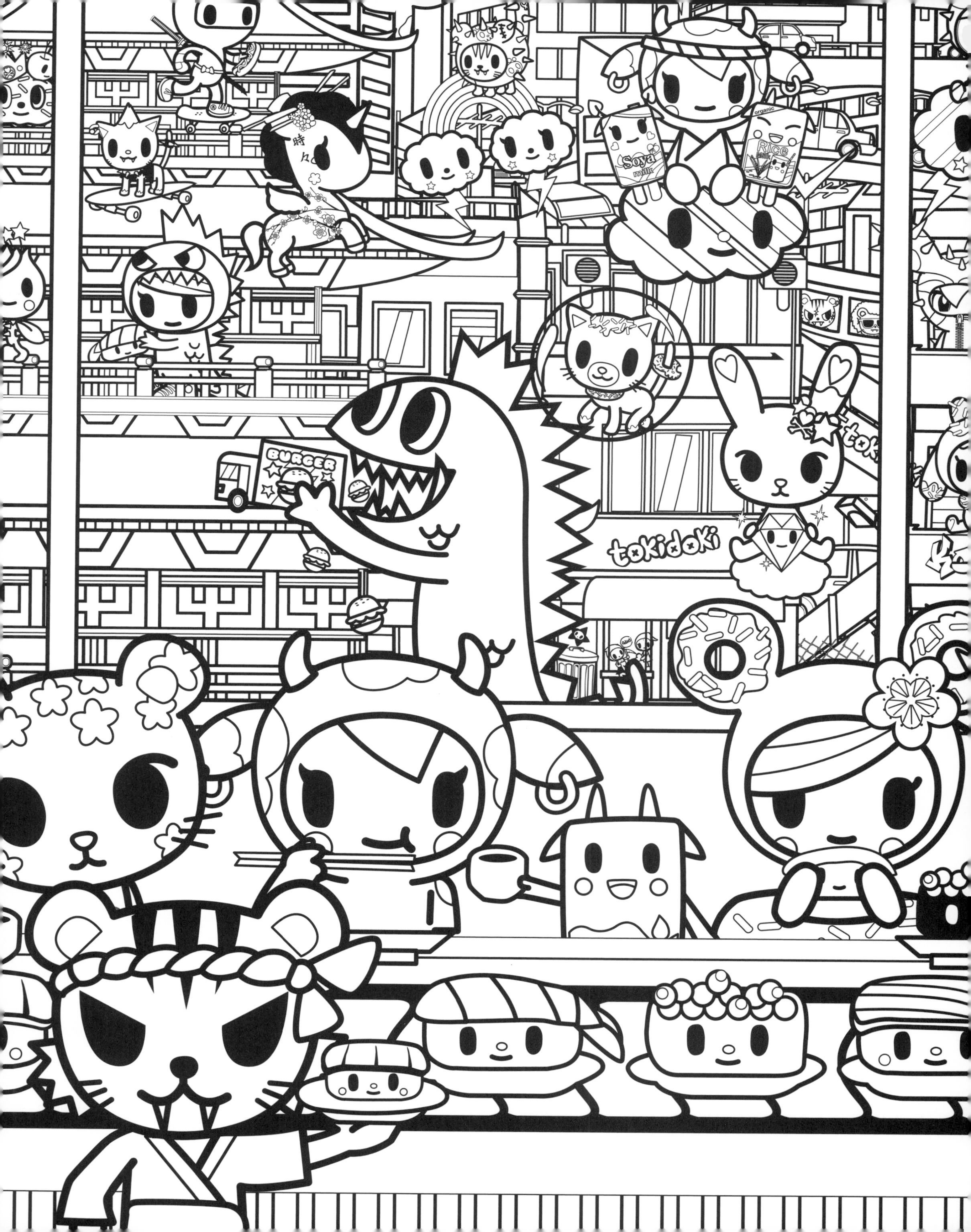
organic
Soya
milk
Rice
milk
BURGER
tokidoki

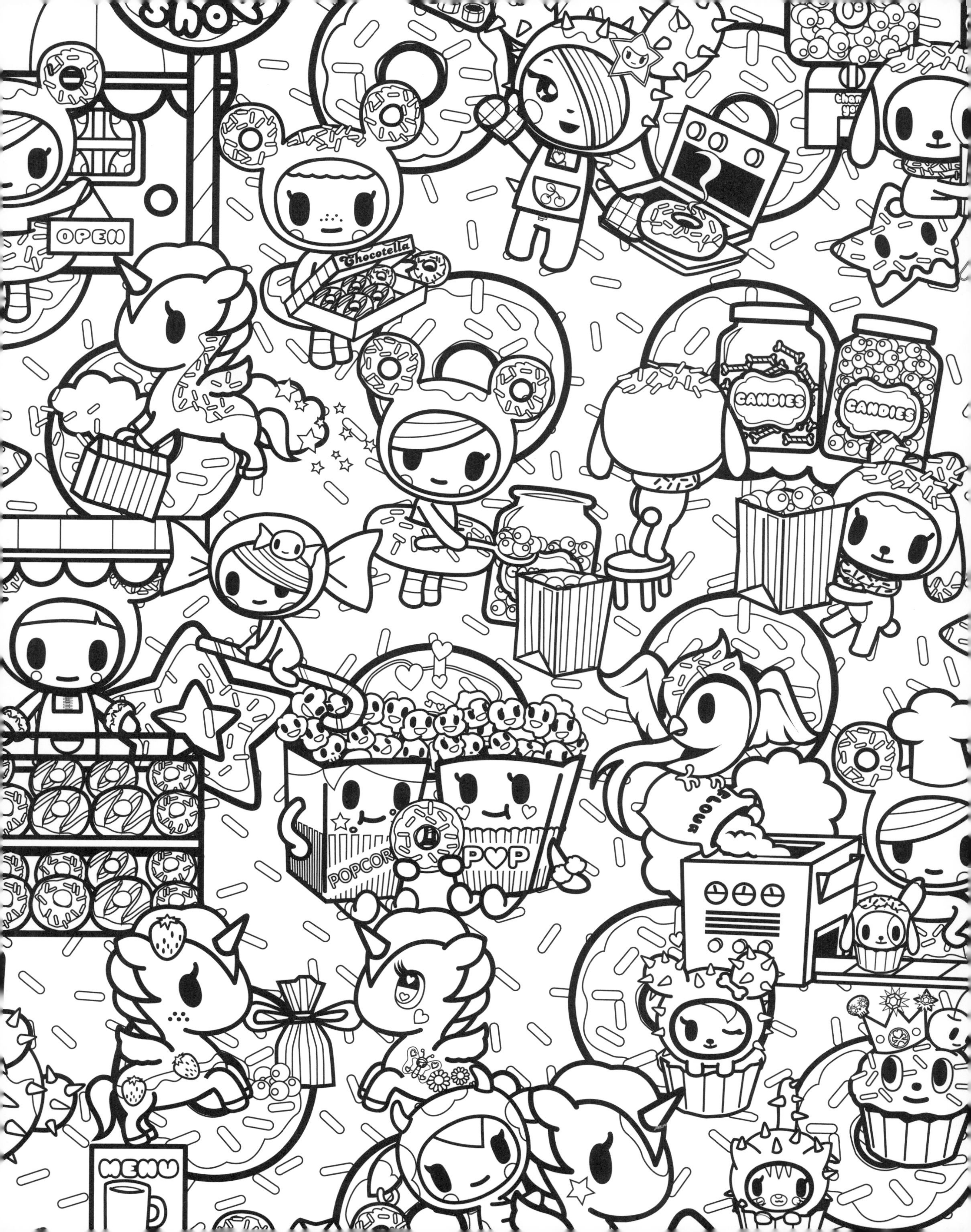
OPEN
Chocotella
CANDIES
CANDIES
POPCOR
P♥P
FLOUR
MENU

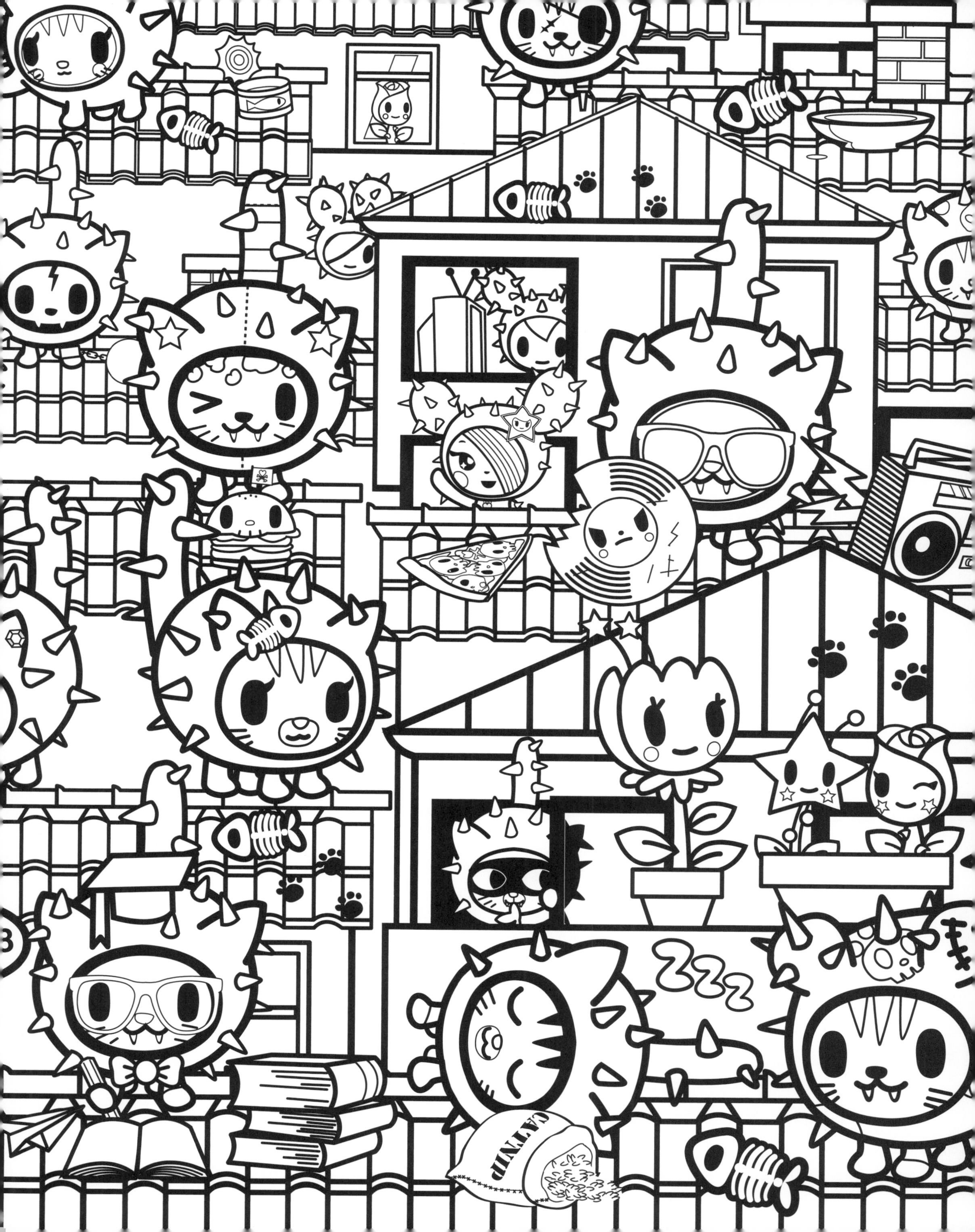
CATNIP

POPCORN
TOKIDOKI DONUTS

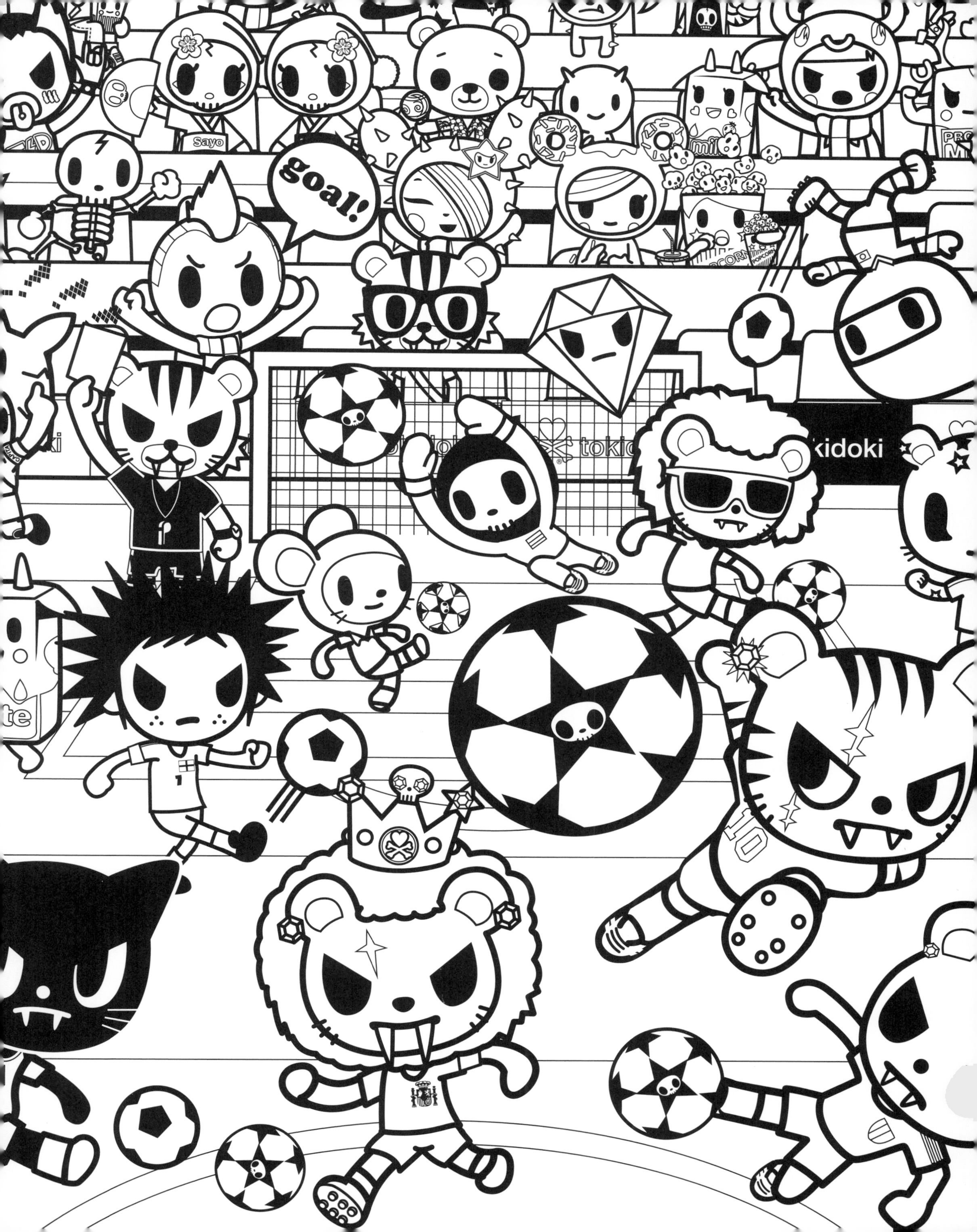

goal!
Sayo
kidoki

TOKIDOKI DONUTS

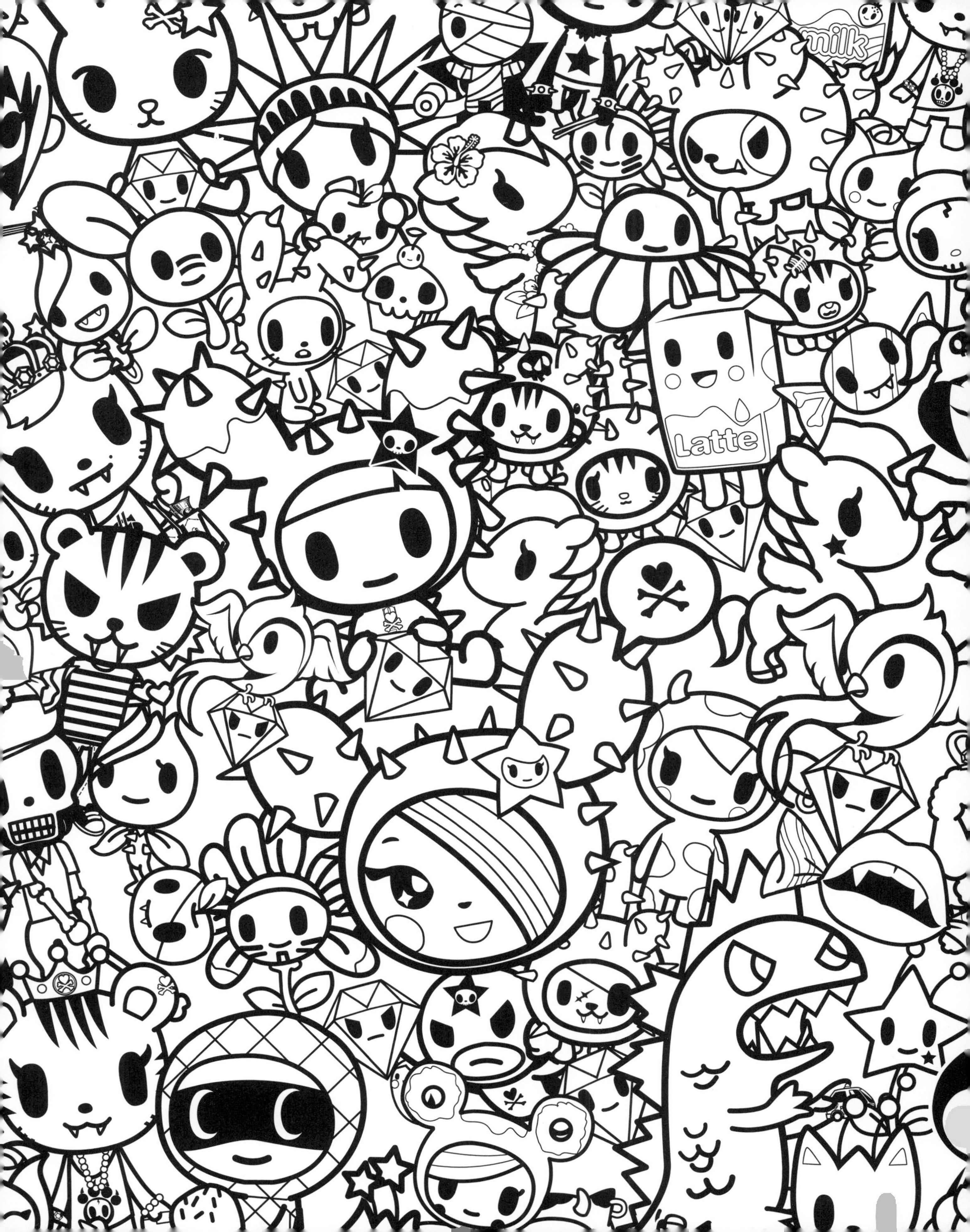
milk
Latte

時々

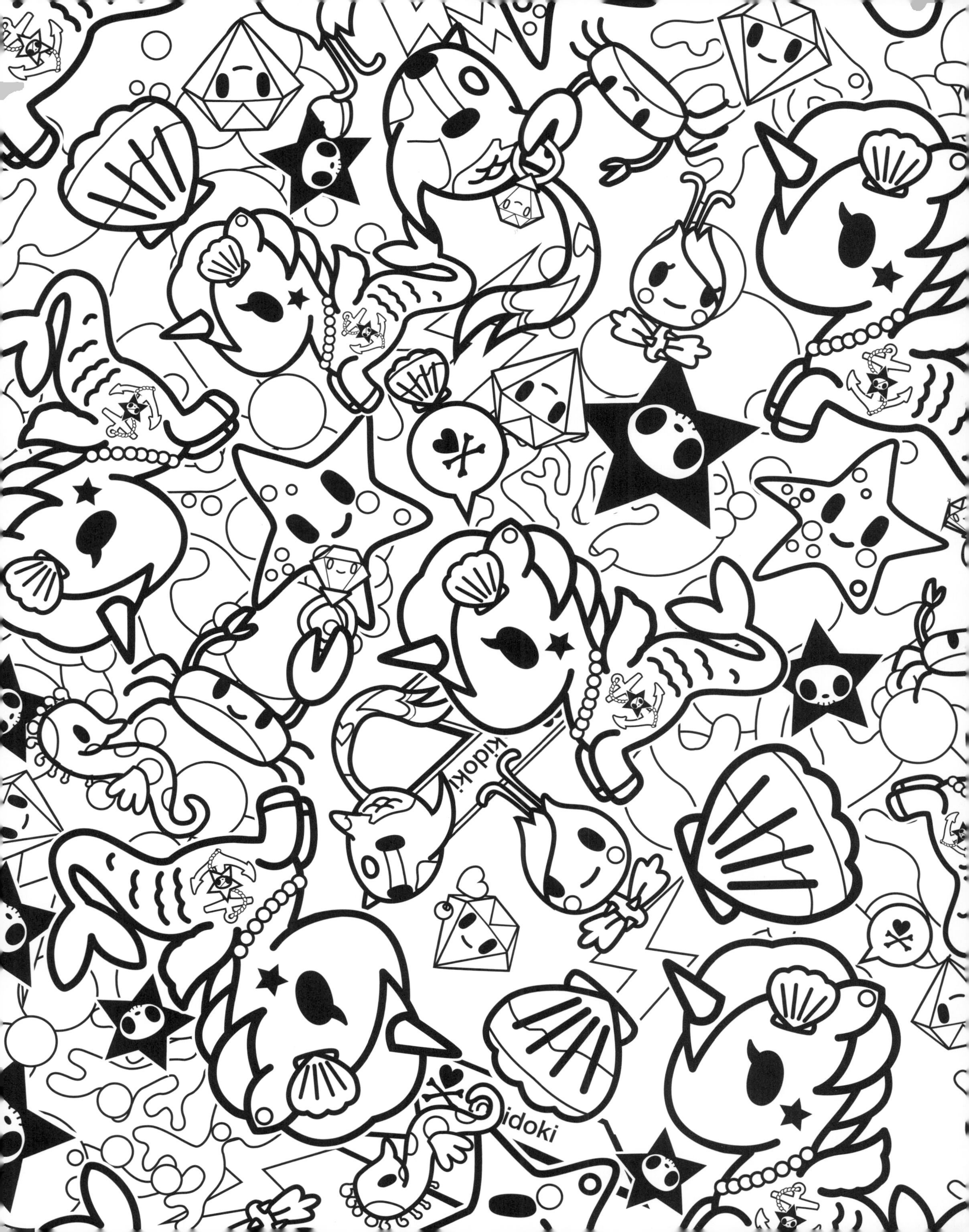
kidoki

Menu
Menu
3rd circle
ciao ciao
ADIO
ciao
stores
TOKIDOKI
latte

tokidoki
POPCORN

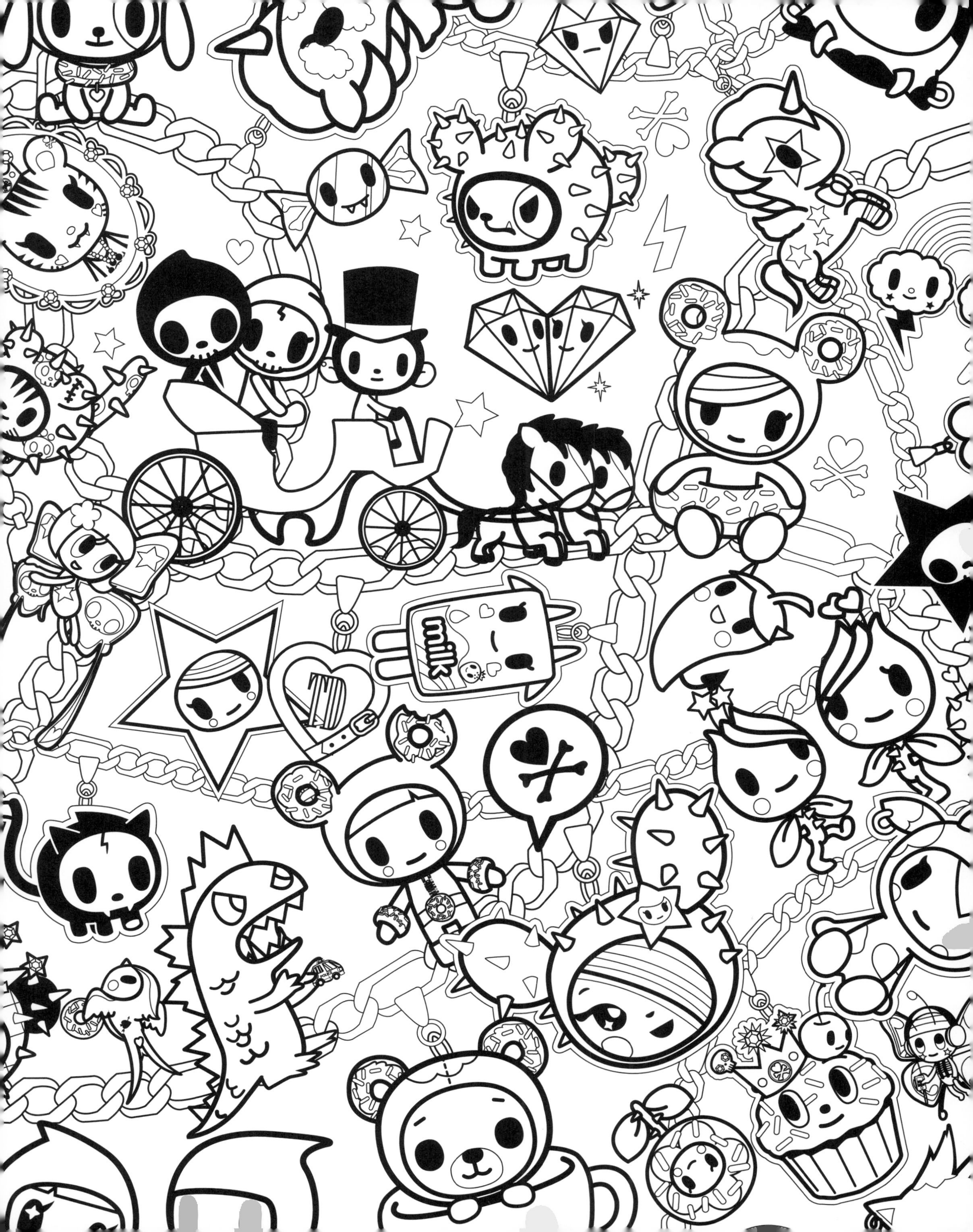
milk

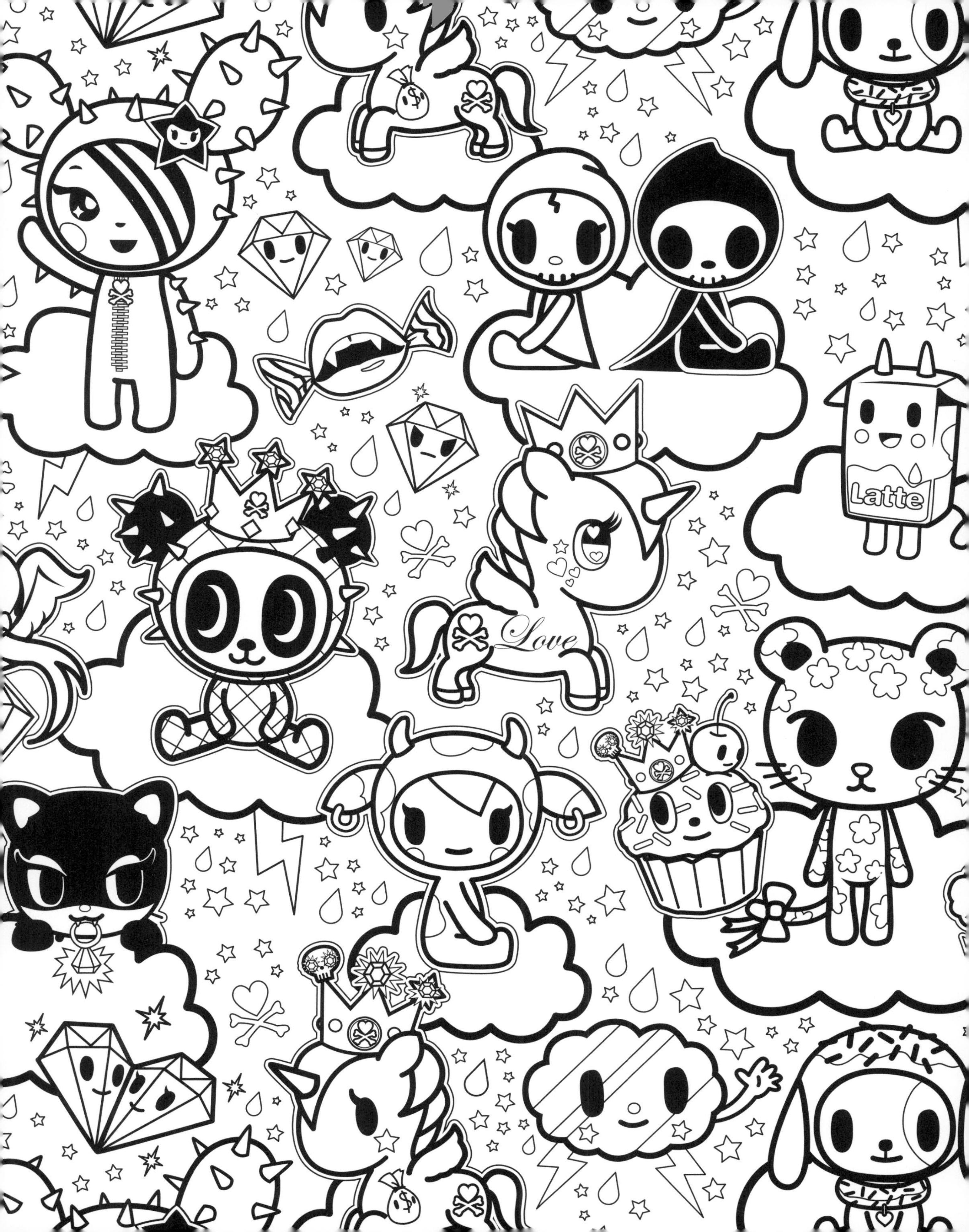
Latte
Love

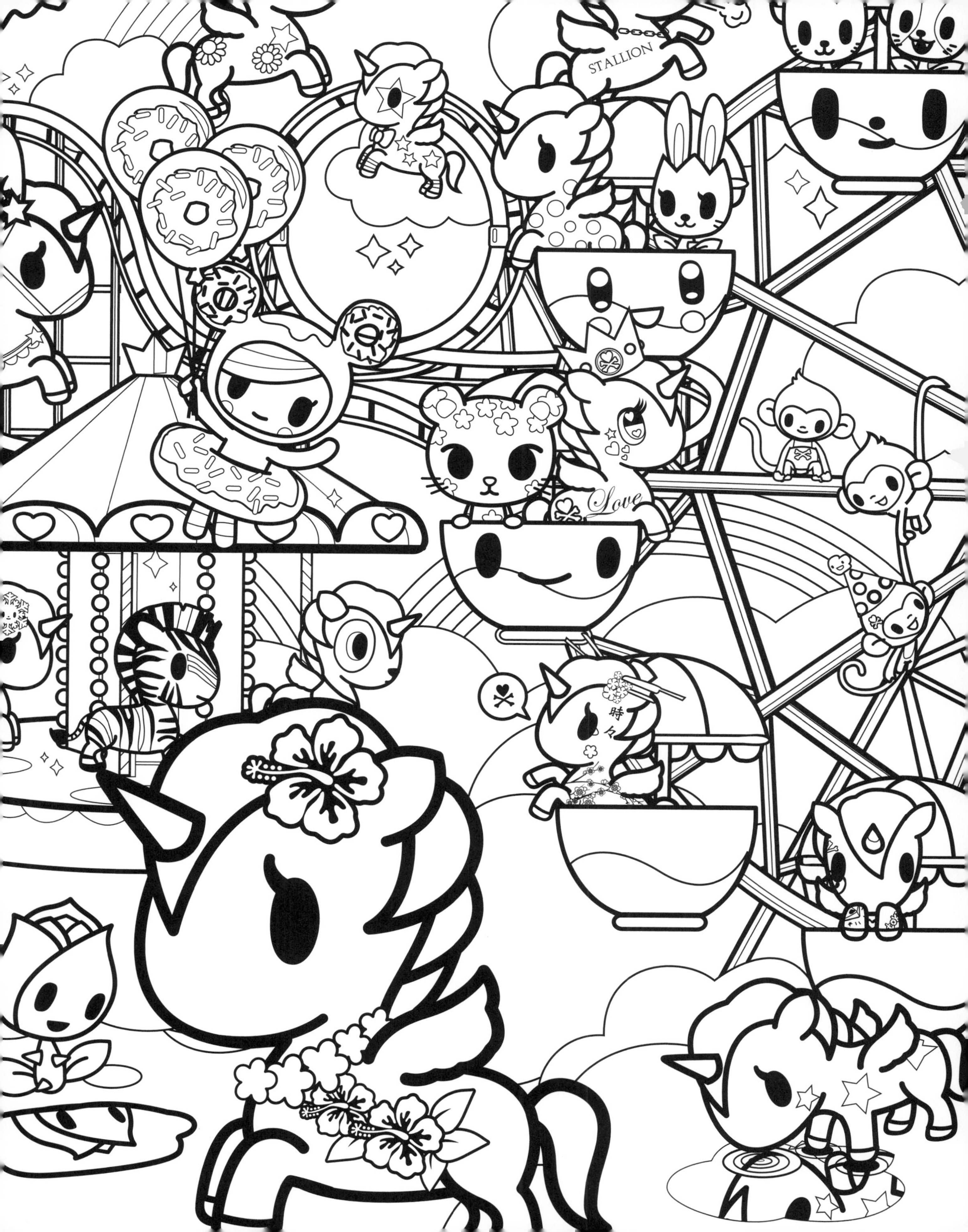
STALLION
Love
時々

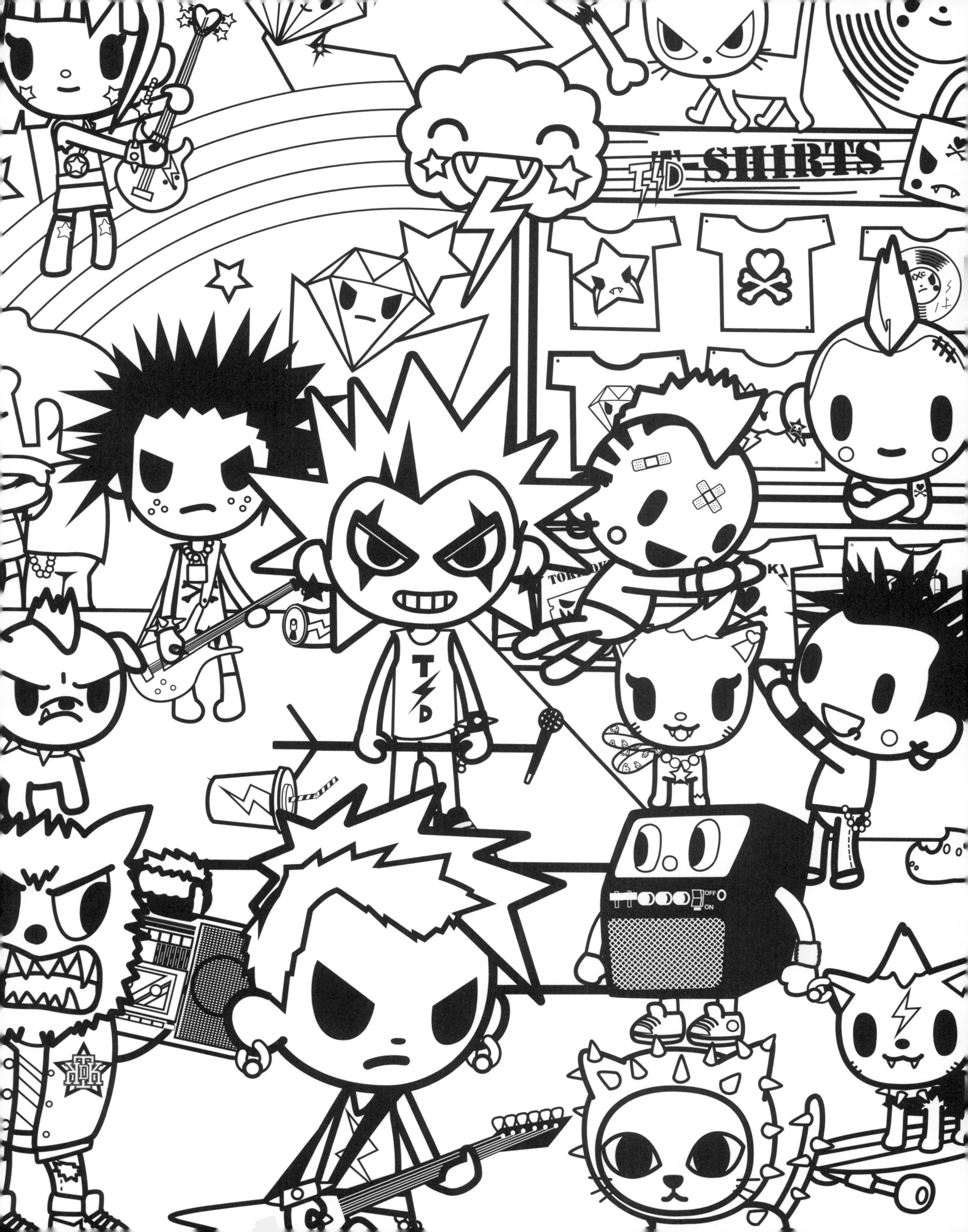

T-SHIRTS
OFF
ON

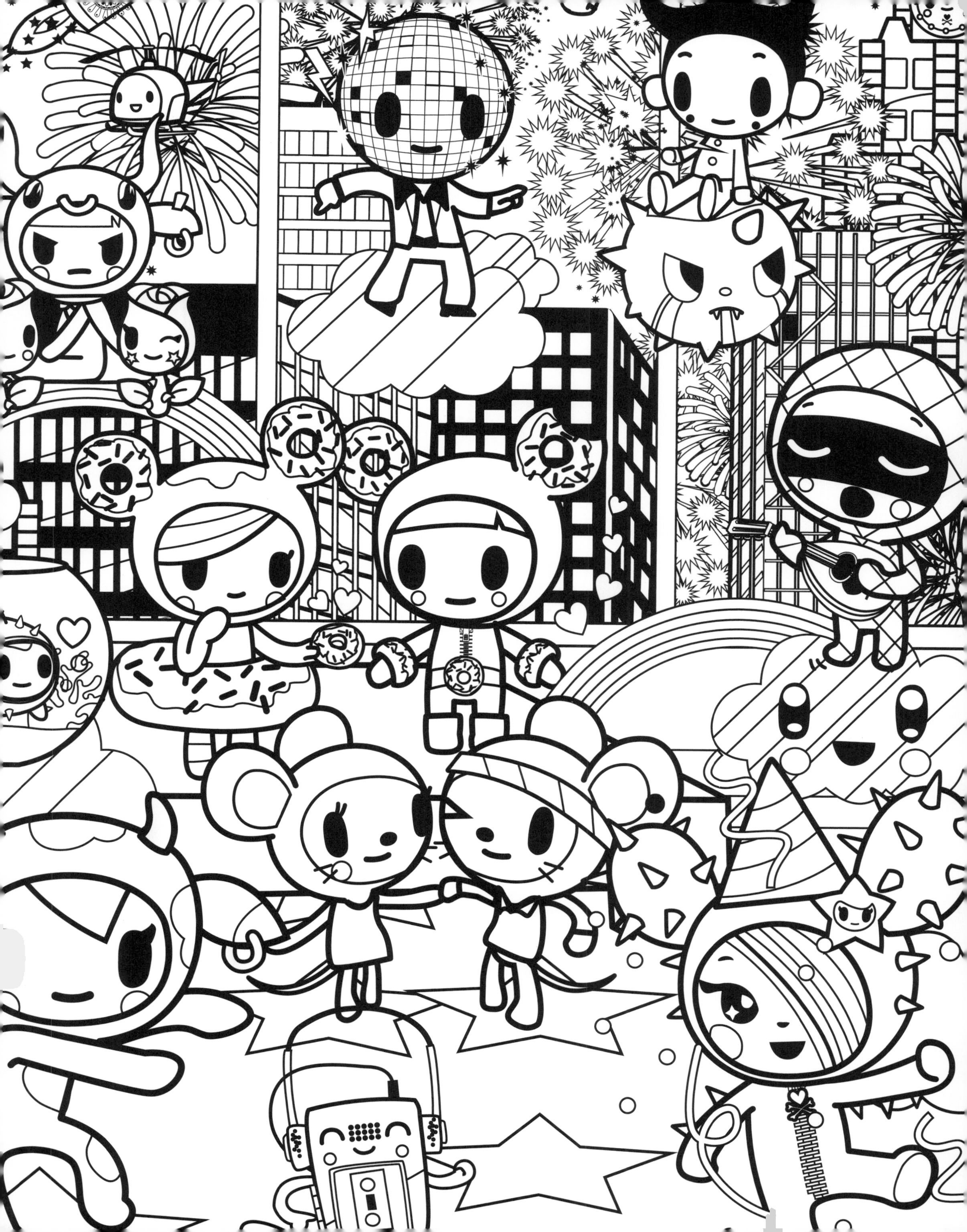

1$1
1$1
POPCORN
CHEESE POPCORN

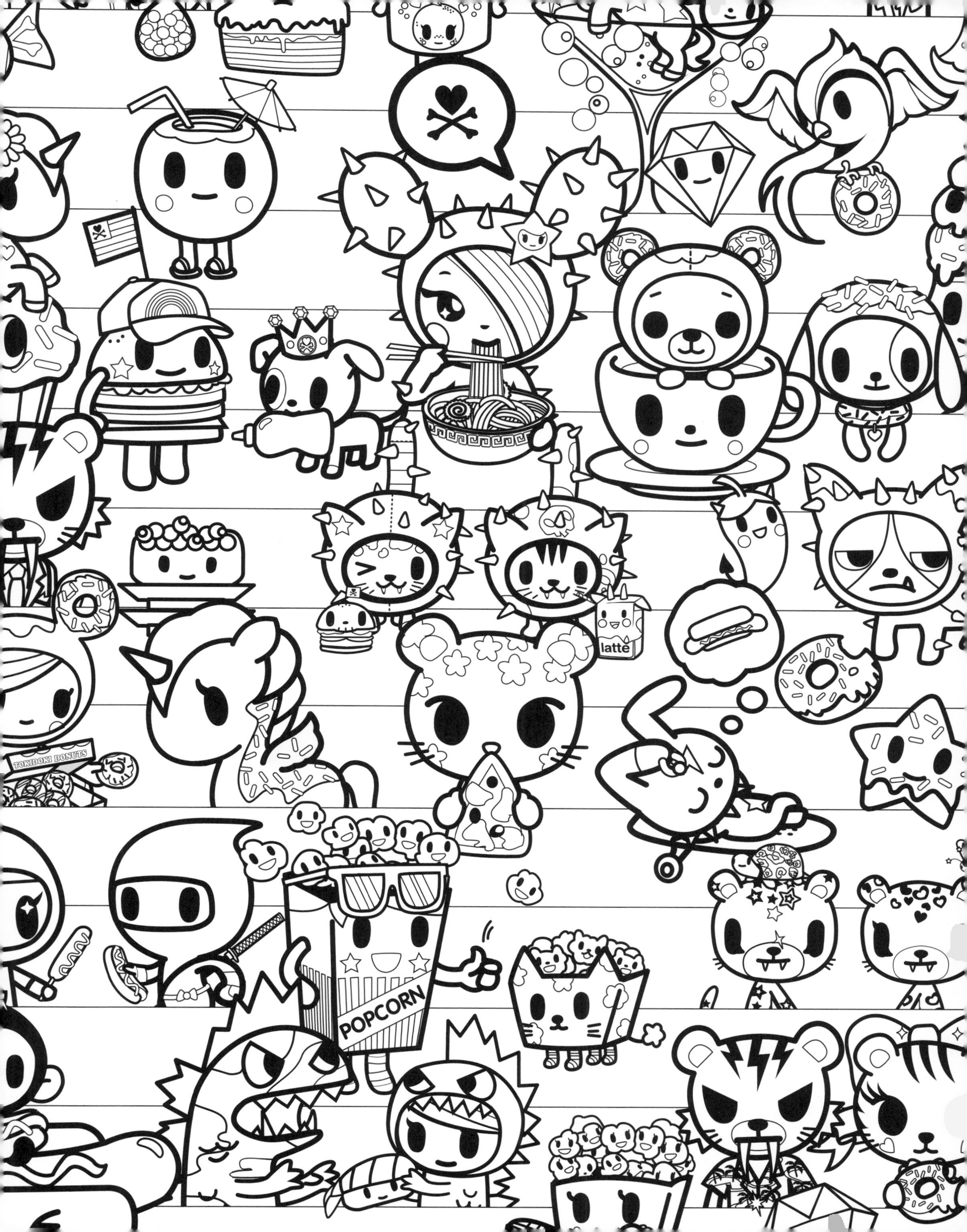
TOKIDOKI DONUTS
latte
POPCORN

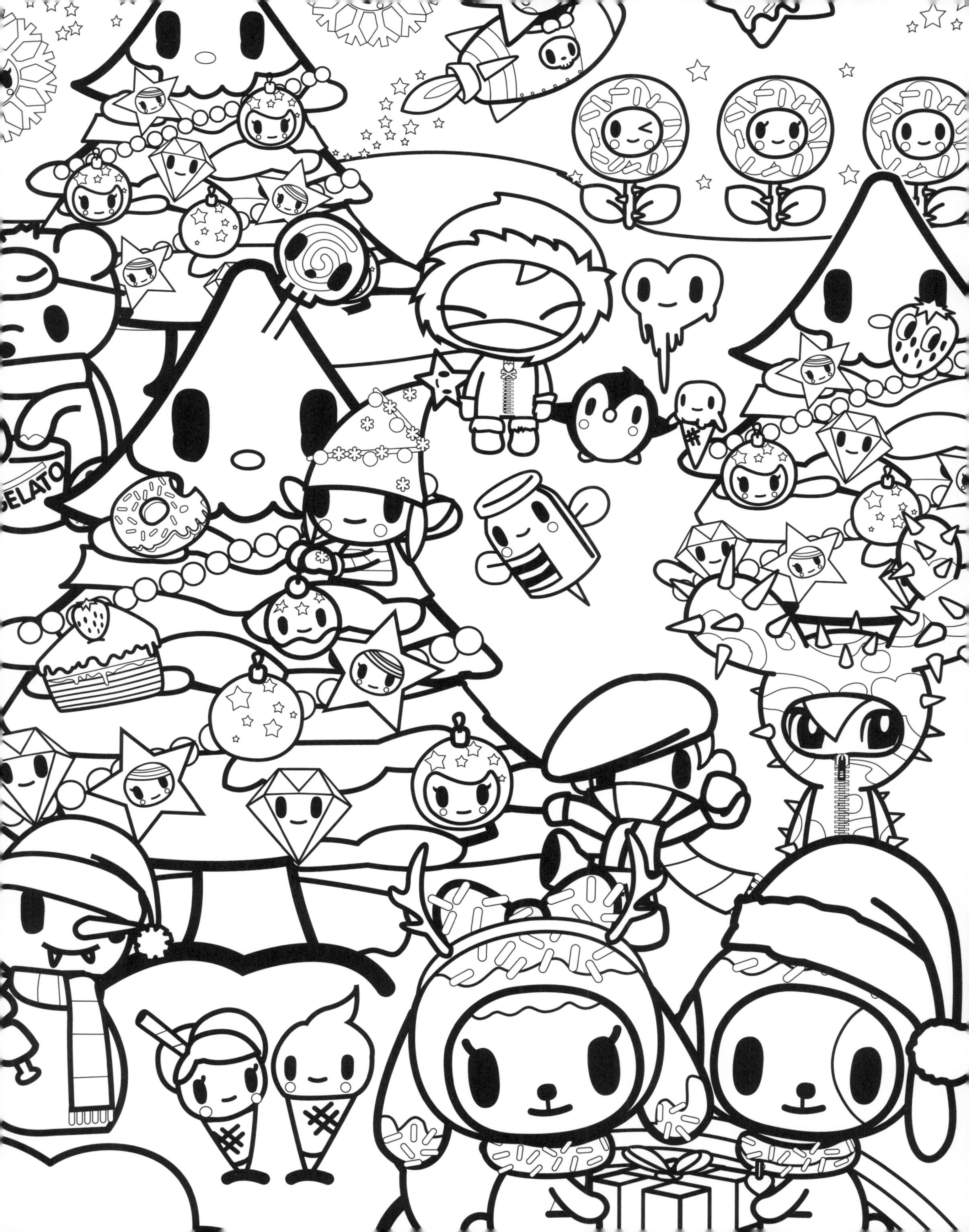
GELATO

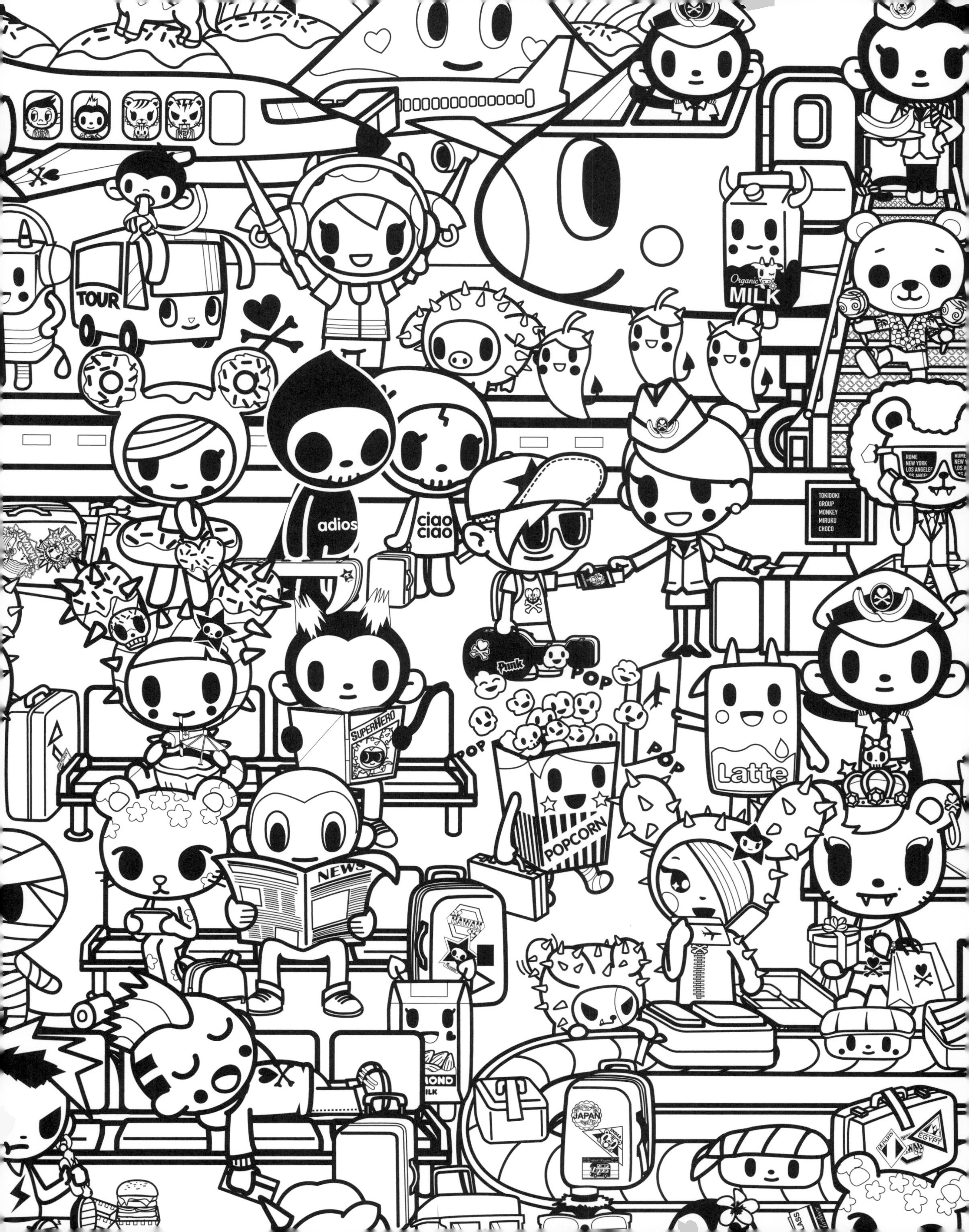
TOUR
Organic
MILK
adios
ciao
ciao
TOKIDOKI
GROUP
MONKEY
MIRUKU
CHOCO
ROME
NEW YORK
LOS ANGELES
Punk
POP
SuperHero
POP
POP
POPCORN
Latte
NEWS
HAWAII
JAPAN
INDIA
EGYPT

POPCORN
Love
milk
YO!
Y

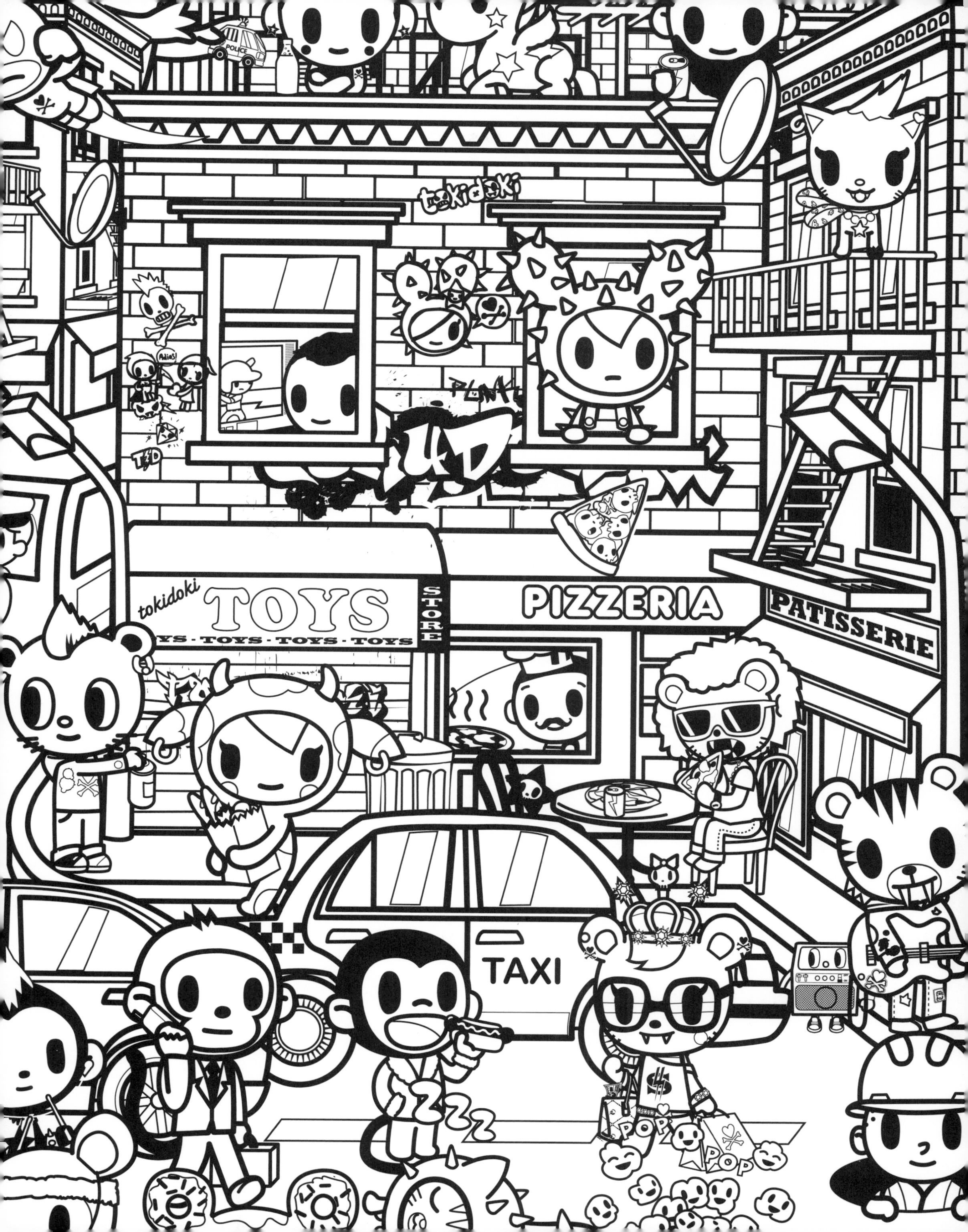
POLICE
tokidoki
Adios!
tokidoki
TOYS
TOYS · TOYS · TOYS · TOYS
STORE
PIZZERIA
PATISSERIE
TAXI
POP
POP

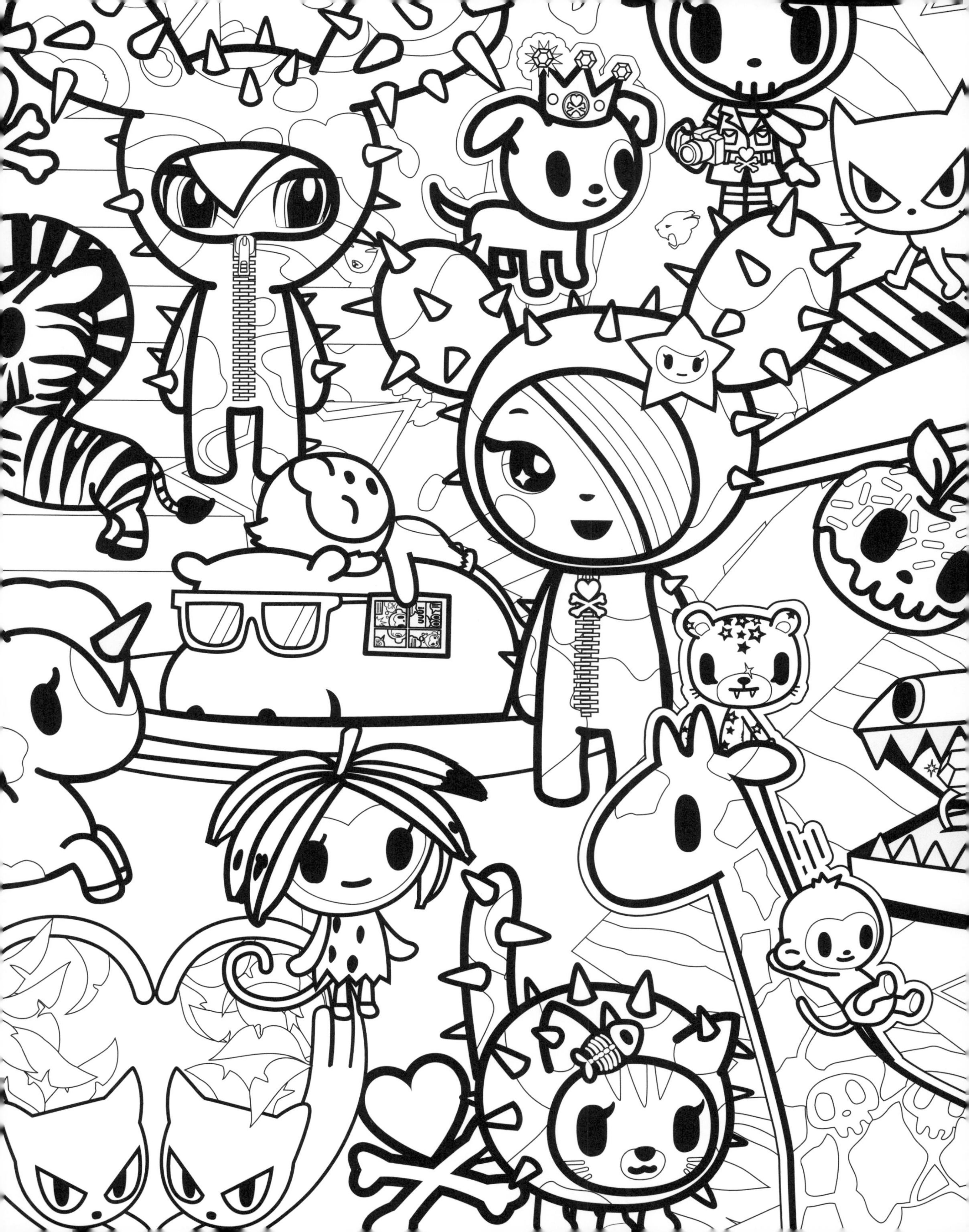

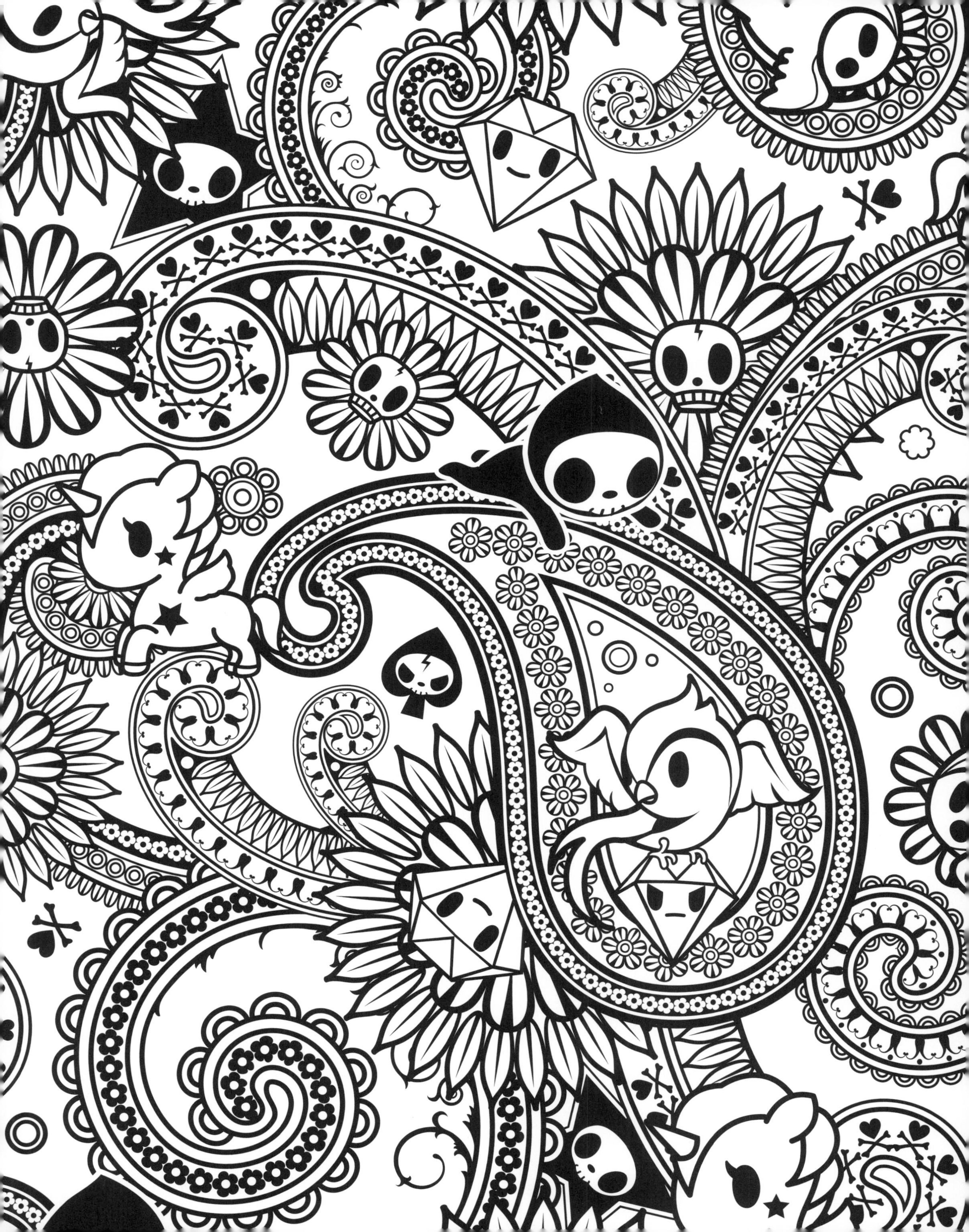

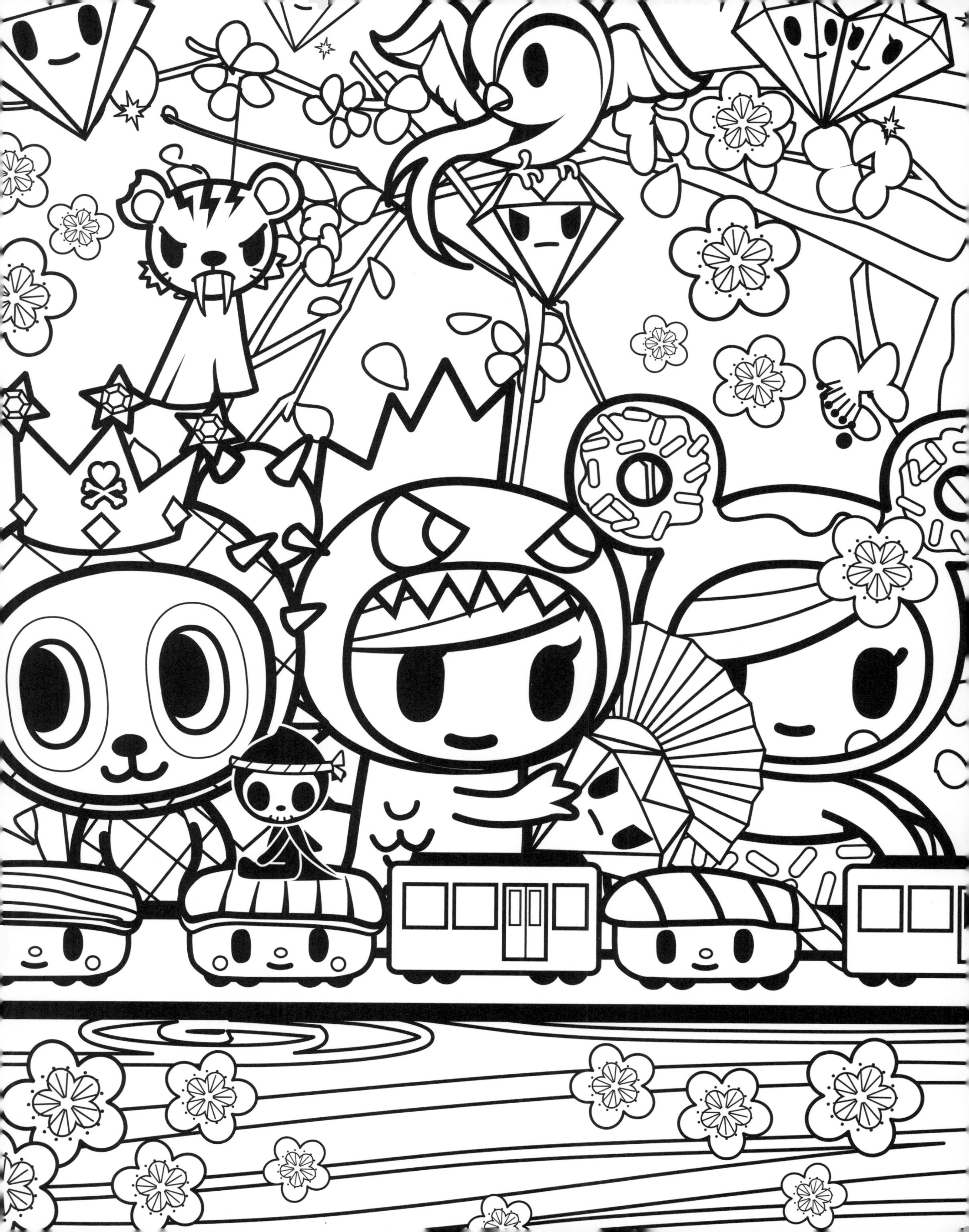

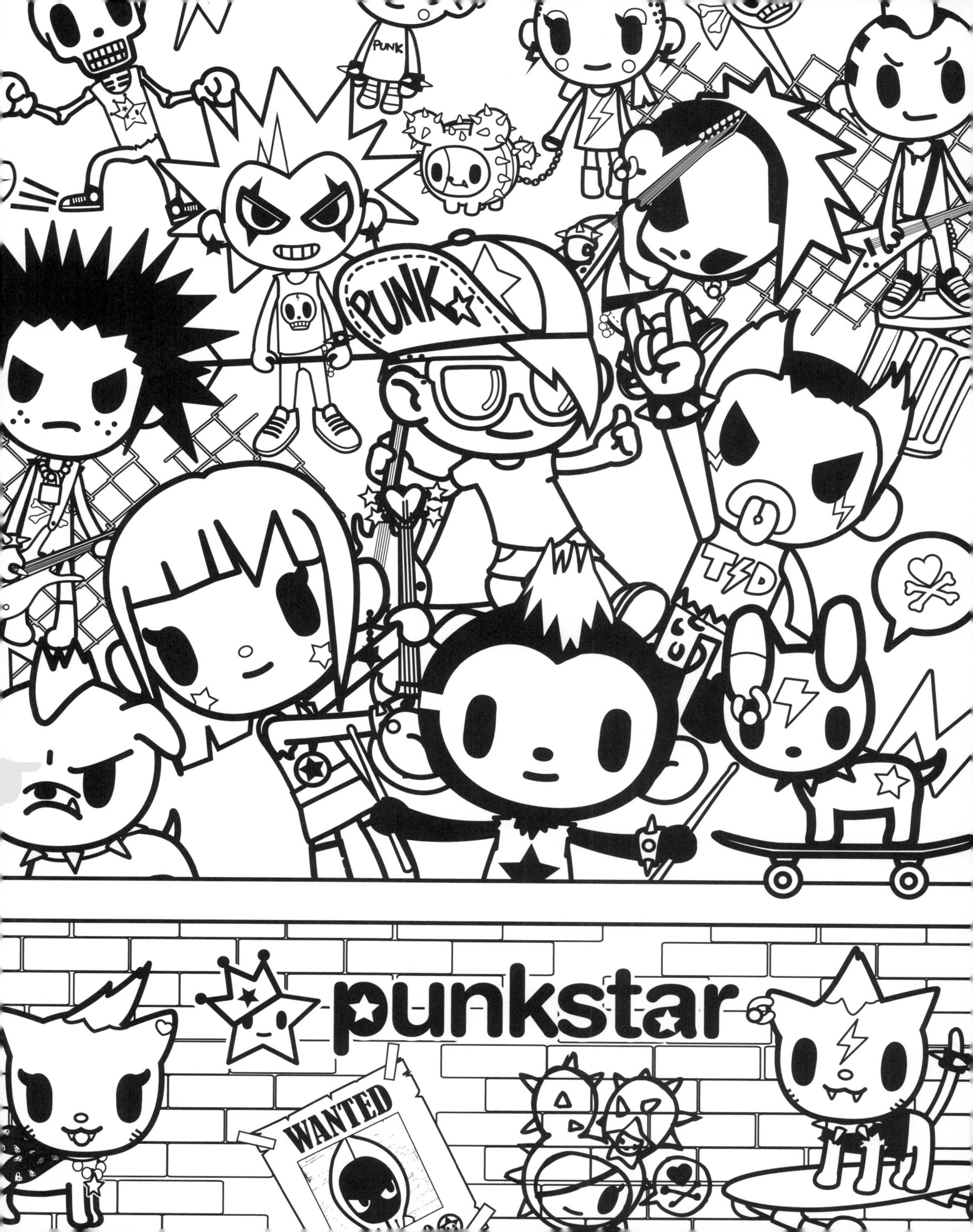
PUNK
PUNK
T/D
punkstar
WANTED

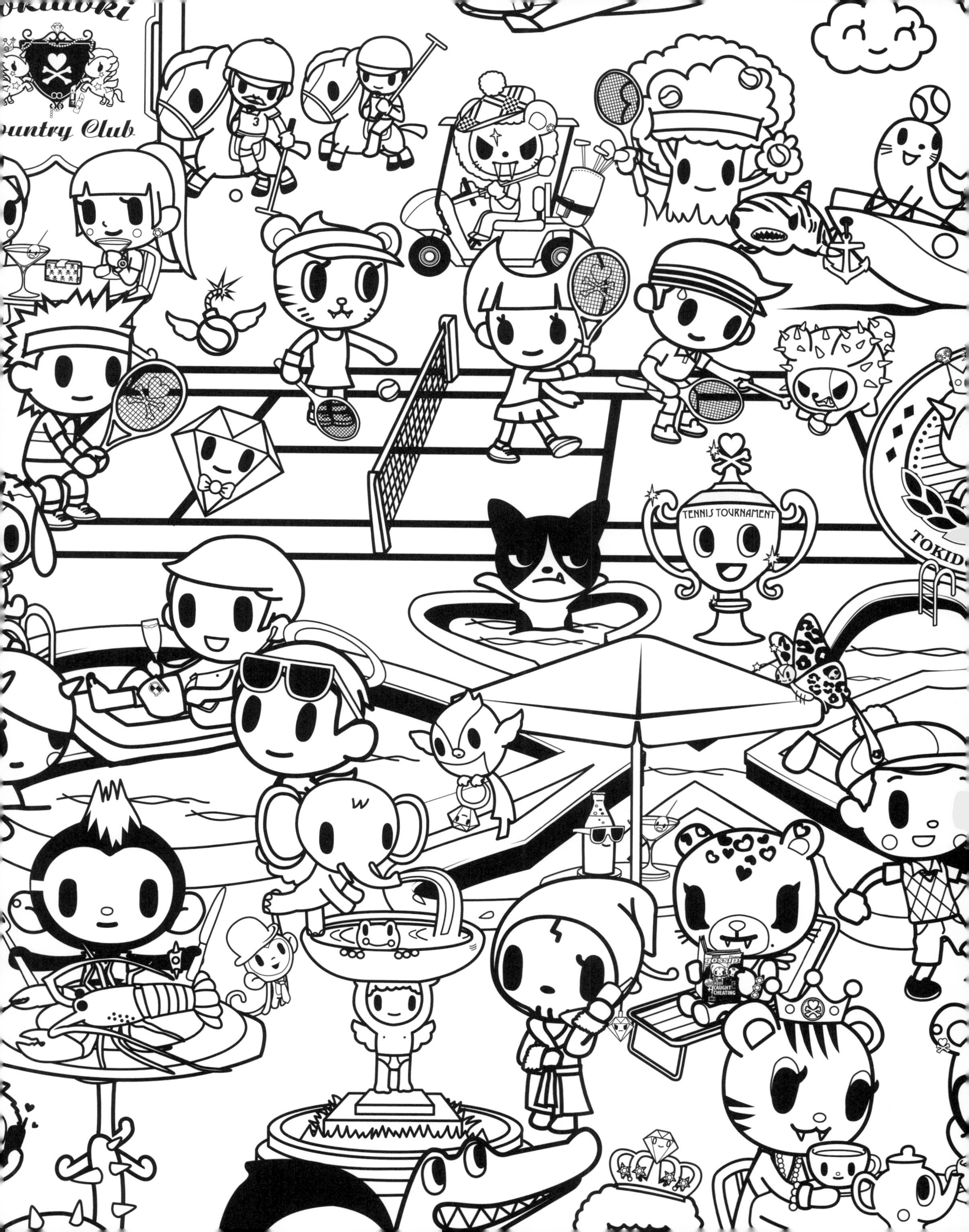

okidoki
ountry Club
TENNIS TOURNAMENT
TOKID
gossip!
CAUGHT CHEATING

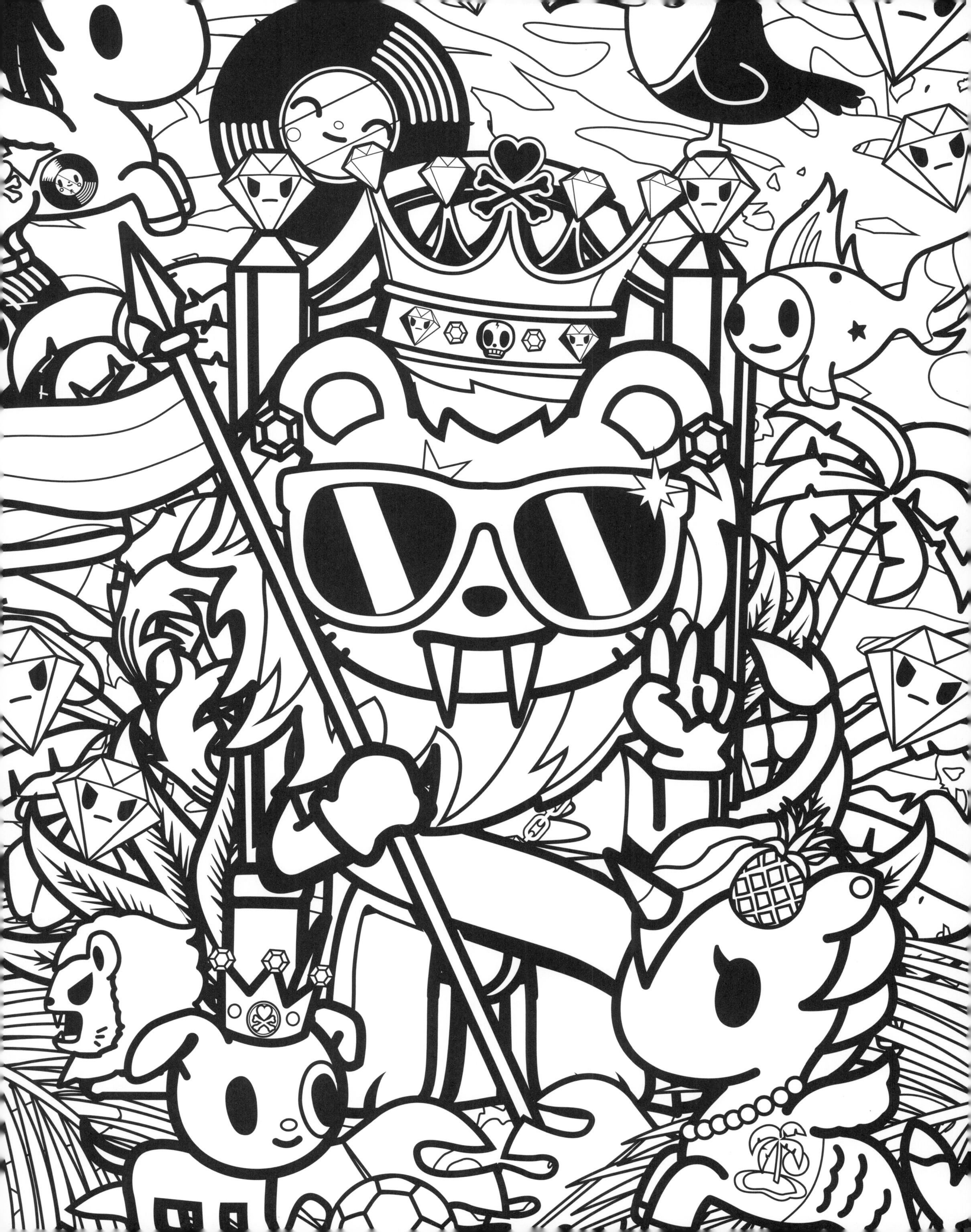

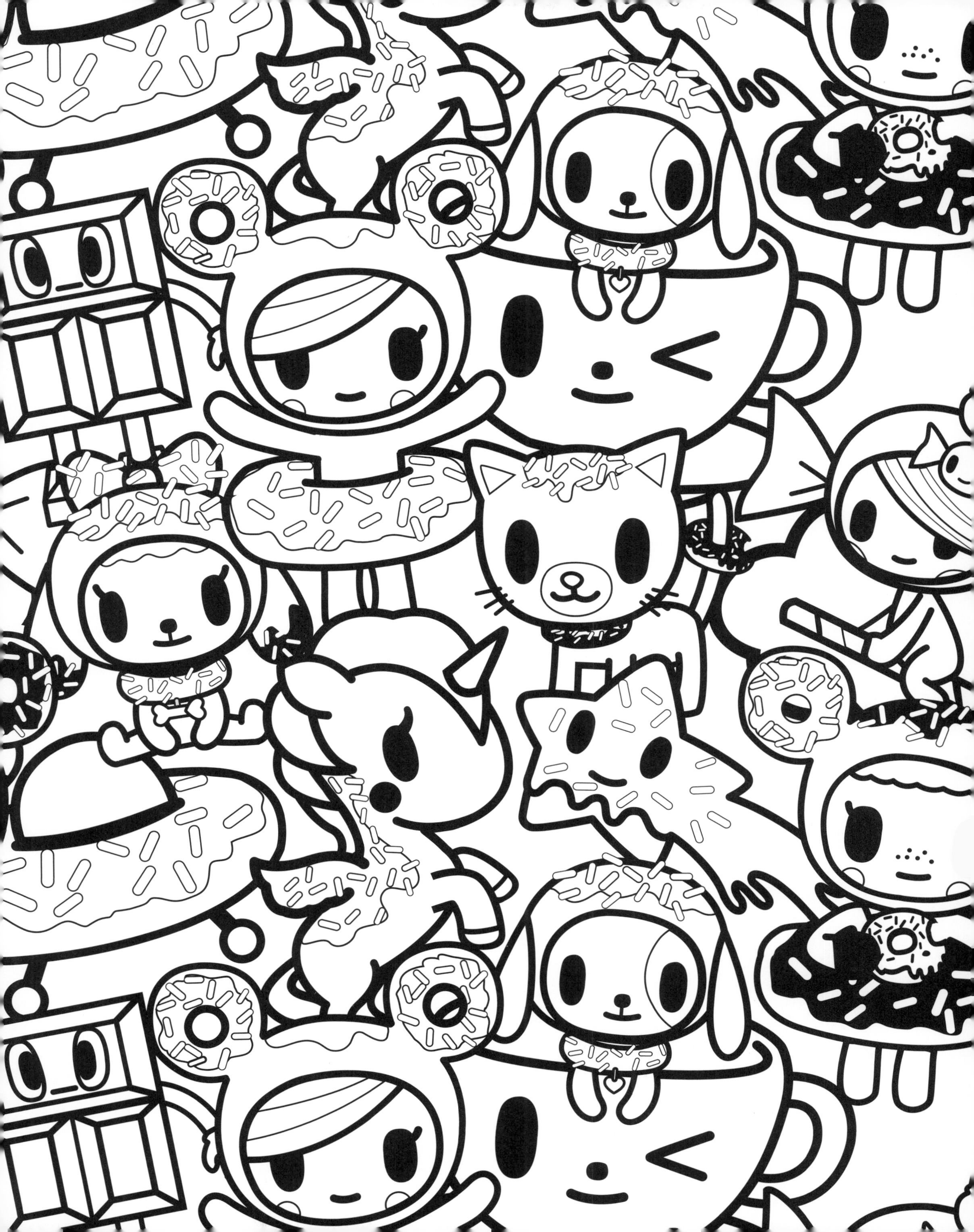

Latte
POPCORN

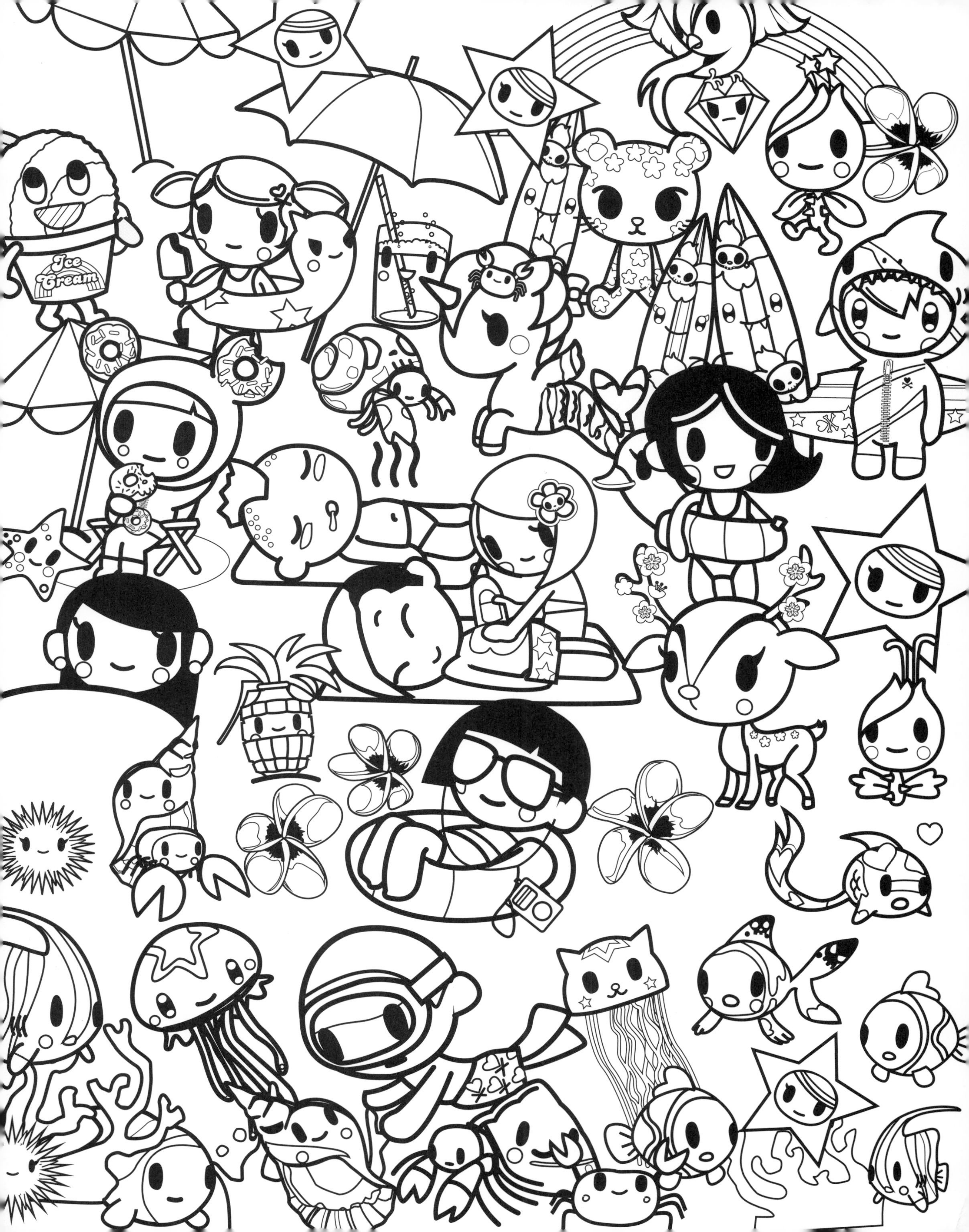
Ice
Cream